)n

# BUY *the* BEACH

## How to Make Millions in Malibu Real Estate

### KATIE BENTZEN

*Buy The Beach Inc.*

Malibu, California
www.buythebeachinc.com

*Buy the Beach: How to Make Millions in Malibu Real Estate*

Copyright © 2005 by Katie Bentzen.

First Edition, 2005
Printed and bound in the United States of America.

Library of Congress Control Number: 2005902681
ISBN: 0-9768621-0-7

Published by Buy the Beach Inc. 23732 Malibu Road,
Malibu, California 90265.

*Production coordinated by Lawrence Ineno*
*Cover design and layout by Nicole Bailon*

Visit our web site at www.buythebeachinc.com to order books or to learn more about Malibu real estate.

*For my husband, Matt.*
*Thank you for always being present to fix any problem, put out any fire,*
*and for being the biggest behind-the-scenes support of Buy the Beach.*

# ACKNOWLEDGEMENTS

S pecial thanks to Lawrence Ineno. Your dedication and expertise have been invaluable to this project.

I would also like to thank the following people for making this book possible: Matt Hansen, Nicole Bailon, Marina Schultz, and Michele Kennedy.

# TABLE OF CONTENTS

# Malibu

1 Las Tunas Beach
5 Carbon Beach
9 Malibu Cove Colony
13 Broad Beach

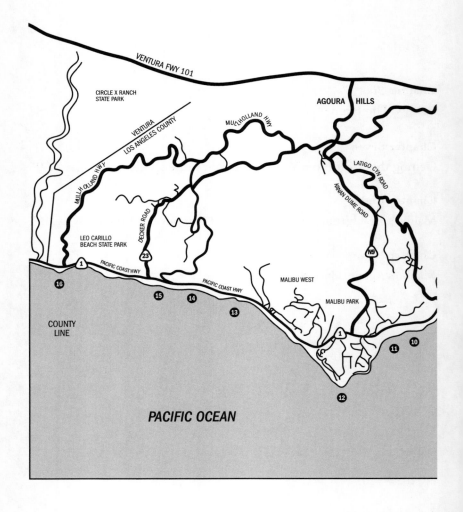

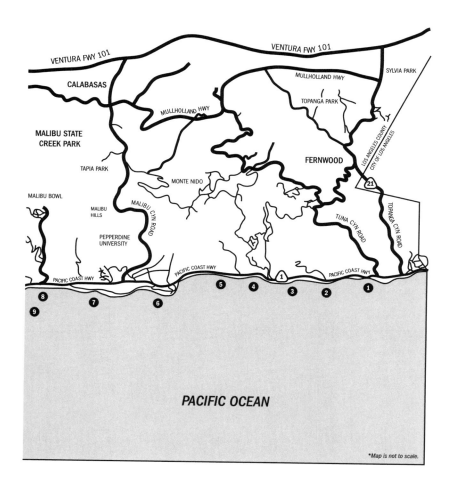

**2** Big Rock Beach  **3** Las Flores Beach  **4** La Costa Beach
**6** Malibu Colony  **7** Malibu Road  **8** Latigo Shore Drive
**10** Escondido Beach  **11** Paradise Cove  **12** Point Dume Bluffs
**14** El Matador Beach  **15** Encinal Bluffs  **16** County Line

*Map is not to scale.*

# INTRODUCTION
*Welcome to Malibu*

An Italian supermodel struts into a La Costa home. The celebrity is accompanied by her entourage: her real estate agent, business manager, and a friend. The seller's agent introduces himself, his greeting is heard above the sound of waves that crash against the coast just a few feet away. The group gathers in the living room as the sun's rays reflect off of the Pacific Ocean and flood the interior space with Southern California light. Suddenly, a bird flies in from the deck. Its wings flutter back and forth feverishly, struggling to find its way to freedom. Unfortunately, any attempt to ascend to the sky is blocked by the plaster ceiling above. The agent panics, fearing that this regrettable event will spoil the celebrity's experience.

Everyone tries to do something—one person runs around in circles, another waves his arms back and forth, and another jumps up to the ceiling—everyone except for the supermodel. On this day, her statuesque height is not only a gift to the runways of Paris, Milan, and Tokyo but also provides a blessing to the suffering bird. She stands still, reaches up to a corner, cups her hand, and gathers the animal in her palm. Then, in an act that would cause Mother Nature to watch with envy, she holds the bird near her bosom, walks to the deck, extends her arms, and frees the feathered creature. Its wings spread as it makes its way toward the heavens.

Welcome to the world of Malibu beachfront real estate. As you'll read throughout this book, Malibu's beachfront definitely lives up to its reputation as being home to the rich and famous. Within these pages, you'll get a look into what it's like to buy and sell homes for Hollywood actors, heirs to multi-million dollar fortunes, and the foreign elite. By reading about what they do, you'll learn how to make millions investing by the beach.

As a Malibu resident for 25 years and a beachfront real estate agent for over 15 years, I'm delighted to share my experience with you. Like most of you, my career journey has had many ups and downs and memorable experiences along the way.

My life in Malibu began in 1980 when my family moved to Malibu from Lake Tahoe, California. When I first arrived, I was a little lost. Malibu is known to be a tight knit community, and when my family and I began our lives here, I felt like an outsider. Fortunately, because of my interest in horses and my status as a stay-at-home mom, I quickly met others who shared the same lifestyle.

While living in Pointe Dume, I acquainted myself with my neighborhood. I recall talking with local horse owners and hearing them express their frustration about the new construction that threatened their trails. Many of these residents believed that they were being pushed out of their communities. Others would complain about their real estate transactions. They told me that their agents were not available when they needed them and weren't acting aggressively enough to sell their homes.

After hearing the concerns of locals and witnessing changes within my neighborhood, I became interested in Malibu real estate. Over the course of eight years, as I raised my children, I knew my community well. I spent time learning about the real estate around me and met the residents who lived in my neighborhood. Then in 1989, I decided to become a real estate agent.

At that time, real estate agents were not as numerous as they are today. This is mainly because there wasn't the lure of making lots of money that is currently bringing so many into this profession. To be hired by a real estate broker at that time, you had to have something to offer—which, in real estate, meant that you had to have a home to sell.

When I started, my desire to get into real estate was certainly there, but all the wishing in the world did little to get me a listing to sell. So I found myself in a difficult situation: I wanted to get my career rolling, but without a home to sell, I couldn't get a job as an agent.

I arranged to interview with a broker in Malibu. When he asked me the inevitable, whether I had a listing to sell, I had to come up with a creative answer. I told him yes—the home my family and I were currently living in. Immediately, I had an expensive Malibu listing, and I got hired.

Now that I was an agent with a home to sell, I needed clients. To generate leads, I began hosting open houses in my home. Every Sunday I would bake chocolate chip cookies, open my door to the Malibu community, and hope for the best. Some Sundays, I would have a plate full of cookies left over because only one person would visit. Other times, I would be glad that I had no visitors because of the strange people who seemed to gravitate into my home that day. Looking back, I recall that on frustrating days, when I didn't feel like I knew what I was doing and sat in my home alone, a visitor would walk in, say something kind and leave. That one person would make the effort worthwhile and would motivate me to continue.

Like many self-starters, I had humble beginnings. In fact, my first year's income was $1,500—and that was not from a sale but a lease. During the week, I went to the real estate office. As a rookie, I was in training to answer the phones. Phone calls were important, even more so than today because there was no Internet or e-mail. Prospective clients would phone the agent to hear details about a listing. Therefore, office "floor time," as they would call it, was critical to generating business—so much so that new real estate agents had to train before answering the phone. Once I was given floor time, I quickly learned how difficult it was to get a phone number, or in other words, a lead.

Initially, I would answer the phone and the caller would ask me questions: What was the square footage of the home? How many bedrooms did it have? What was the price? And how was the neighborhood? I would answer all the caller's questions, thank them for their time, and say good-bye.

In that instance, I had provided the caller with important information, yet I had no phone number to call him back with. It took me some time to begin pursuing the phone number more aggressively. As you can probably imagine, the difficulty was in requesting the number. Part of me was afraid of hearing no, which prevented me from asking. Meanwhile, I would listen to my top-producing colleagues communicate on the phone and zoom in and out of the office with their clients. At that point, I knew that I needed to learn from them.

After a while, when a caller would contact me, I began answering the phone call more skillfully. If someone were interested in a type of home that I didn't have listed, I would respond with, "I think I saw something that fits your description. If you don't mind, could you provide me with your phone number and I'll get right back with you?"

Now, the person on the other end of the phone would give me her phone number. Then after the phone conversation, I would do my research, and always, without exception, I would find a property that fit her description.

Over the course of months, my floor time skills improved to the point that my broker began taking notice. He eventually asked me to train others on effective floor time communication. I began teaching classes on how to respond to inquiries, create rapport over the phone, and get the caller's contact information.

Meanwhile, on Sundays, I continued to hold open houses at home. One day, the vice president of Playboy Magazine came to visit. He and his wife were impressed that I was there the same day every week. I remember him complimenting me on being such a hard worker.

The couple had a home for sale. They told me that they wished that their agent would regularly hold open houses and bake cookies for their visitors. "When your listing expires," I recall telling them, "give me a call."

Like many buyers and sellers of real estate, the vice president wanted his real estate agent to host weekly open houses where anyone off the street could take a look at the house. The reality is, open houses do little to sell a home. In fact, the percentage of homes sold through an open house is in the single digits. Instead, what open houses do is spread a real estate agent's name throughout a community. Many residents attend open houses, and this is an effective way for agents to build relationships with neighbors.

The next Sunday, the vice president's wife came to visit me again at my open house. This time she brought along a recipe for chocolate chip cookies. She really enjoyed mine and thought that I would appreciate trying something new. After receiving the recipe, I baked a batch; the cookies were excellent.

During another Sunday open house, Thomas Gottschalk, a German talk show host, came to visit. Later, a colleague told me that he was the "Jay Leno of Germany." He lived in the neighborhood, and after seeing my weekly open houses, he finally decided to stop by. While he was there, his friend came for a visit as well; I immediately recognized this person from his American action films.

Thomas told me that he had come all the way to Malibu from Germany, and he was disappointed that he didn't live on the beach. At that moment, I let him know that I saw a fantastic beachfront property that he might be interested in seeing.

I took the talk show host to the home, and he immediately wanted to buy it. He purchased it for $5 million—an unheard of price on Malibu's beachfront at the time. That sale, and a couple of others, made me one of the top producers in my office. Over the next eight years, I represented him in the purchase of five more homes.

Eventually, the vice president of Playboy contacted me and wanted me to sell his home. When he hired me as his real estate agent, I held open houses at his residence just like I did in mine—every week I opened the front door and offered guests freshly baked cookies.

As I mentioned earlier, when I started in real estate, the industry had far less agents than it has today. And as a new agent, I was considered a nobody. But because the vice president of Playboy and his wife were pleased with my work, they referred Hugh Heffner to me.

Over the next couple of years, I slowly started building a client base. At first, when one of my buyers wanted to see a home, I would call the seller's real estate agent and schedule a showing. Most of the time, because my name wasn't well known throughout the real estate community, I had to give detailed facts about my clients and me. Real estate agents were careful whom they were going to show their multi-million dollar homes to. Therefore, they screened potential buyers and their agents.

But with clients like Hugh Heffner and German celebrities, I gained instant credibility. Eventually, many of my clients were contacting me to purchase second homes on Malibu's beachfront, and this is how I began specializing in coastal property. During this time, Malibu's real estate trends were changing—residents began living in their beachfront properties as vacation homes rather than their primary residences.

Meanwhile, I continued to meet high-profile clients through the open houses. The brother of a famous actor came to visit one day. He wasn't interested in purchasing beachfront property. What brought him through the door was his interest in seeing what a beachfront house looked like. I engaged him in conversation and asked him what kind of home he was looking for. He told me that he wanted to buy a ranch. I shared that there was a home in escrow that looked like the one he described. After seeing the home for himself, he bought it.

In addition, I attended many open houses to learn more about real estate. I recall one open house I visited. I pretended to be a buyer looking for a home in the neighborhood. The listing agent was an older gentleman. I looked around and told him that I thought the house was lovely. He was gracious and gave me a tour. We spent about thirty minutes talking and looking through the home. In the end, I asked for his business card, but he didn't bother to ask for any contact information from me. Considering that homes are rarely sold through an open house, I was surprised that he did not even ask for my phone number.

Experiences like these taught me valuable lessons about the real estate business.

For the first couple of years in my career, I realized the importance of persistence. I also learned to focus on the long term when setting out to reach goals. After all, immediate success was not what kept me sitting alone in my home on Sundays surrounded by chocolate chip cookies. Even today, I'll contact buyers interested in Malibu's beachfront for years before they decide to purchase a home. One client is a CFO of a Hollywood studio. I met him three years ago. Although I knew a sale wouldn't happen right away, his commitment to live by the beach was clear. I phoned him whenever something interesting was for sale, which was about once every three months. Three years later, he found his dream home, and I represented him in the purchase.

When I finally started to have a solid client base, I realized what my strengths were and developed them. The key for me was having a good feel for people and creating solid rapport with clients. I hold very strong to the belief that if you're honest and knowledgeable, then anyone looking for a home in any price range will be confident that you'll take good care of her.

Malibu's allure is what first brought me here from Lake Tahoe 25 years ago, and my love of the beachfront has kept me here since. Contained within these pages are my 15 years of experience working with Malibu real estate. You'll read stories of clients with whom I've worked as well as stories from my friends and colleagues. Whether you own a Malibu beach home or plan to do so in the future, this book will guide you through the process of buying and selling in one of the best places to live in the world.

# BROKERS AND AGENTS
*Malibu's Real Estate Scene*

Your real estate agent and the brokerage that your agent represents are key factors in making your home purchase a smooth and satisfying process. Therefore, the right broker and agent will make the difference between a beachfront investment that will give you years of pleasure, not to mention a great return on your investment, and one that will make your life miserable.

There are several reasons why buyers and sellers of real estate need to carefully select their real estate agents. One explanation is that in recent years, the nation's most prominent brokerages have been facing more legal challenges than ever before. What complicates matters is that some quickly settle out of court. This means that a homebuyer who uses a brokerage that is known to resolve legal battles out of court, no matter how frivolous the suit, could be at risk. In this chapter, you'll learn the basics about brokers, agents, and big versus small real estate companies.

## BROKERS AND AGENTS

First of all, a real estate broker is a professional who is licensed to own a real estate company. Although some brokers own their own agencies, many work for a company. In addition, a broker is qualified to represent the buyer or seller in a real estate transaction.

A real estate agent is an associate of the broker. A licensed real estate agent who isn't a licensed broker must work under a broker. He or she is qualified to represent buyers and sellers of real estate but cannot work independently of a broker.

Real estate brokers are often affiliated with names of companies you most likely recognize, such as RE/MAX, Prudential, Century 21, Coldwell Banker, and many more. Some brokers own independent real estate companies with names that are well known within a community but don't have national recognition. Because the focus of this book is on beachfront property, the independent and nationally recognized real estate agencies to which I refer will be related to beachfront real estate in Malibu. I make this distinction because there are many independent real estate companies that have their businesses in areas outside of this city.

## DO I CHOOSE A GOOD BROKER, AGENT, OR BOTH WHEN I'M BUYING A HOME?

Selecting a good broker is similar to selecting a good law firm. A prestigious law firm has built its reputation after years of providing quality service to its clients. It has won many high-profile cases, hires the best attorneys, and boasts a wide range of resources. In addition, it is well known in the community, and many of its clients come through referral.

A good agent is like having a good lawyer represent you. With a good lawyer, you may not know much about the firm she works for, but you know that she is an expert in her field. She has a high success rate in her cases, and she treats her clients with respect.

In an ideal real estate transaction, you should have confidence in the broker and the agent who are working for you. But what if you don't know anything about the broker but trust the agent, or vice versa? For instance, imagine that you've been working with an agent for years. Over the course of time she has done a great job representing you. Perhaps she's done such good work that you never even bothered to find out who her broker is.

In the past, I would suggest that this was reason enough to stick with your agent. But with the rise in real estate-related lawsuits, you must be even more careful when you decide whom you'll work with. Legal battles, especially in high stakes Malibu real estate, are becoming more and more common. If you want to stay out of court battles, your best bet is to first, follow the law; second, and equally important, work with an agent who does the same. This is not to say that all agents or brokerages that get involved in court cases are unethical—sometimes lawsuits are unavoidable. To keep yourself protected, however, make sure your agent and broker don't have a track record of lawsuits.

In the event that you know the broker but don't know the agent who will represent you, here is what you need to know. First, if the broker is someone you have known for years, most likely she will refer you to someone that will represent you well. The rule of thumb is that good brokers hire good agents. Once again, think about a prestigious law firm. The founding partner will not risk the reputation on which he has built his practice by hiring mediocre attorneys. The same goes for the broker of a well-known real estate office.

In addition, make sure that the brokerage hasn't been involved in many court battles. The big firms are being sued like never before. You want to make sure that the company that is handling your transaction isn't a magnet for people prepared to sue.

## BROKERS: BIG VERSUS SMALL

Beachfront property is a specialized niche of the real estate market. Even within Malibu, its beachfront has a cachet that separates it from landside property. The basic law of supply and demand is playing out—the amount of coastal property available is far less than the amount of people who want to buy it. This scarcity makes it highly prized and competitive. Therefore, you must be selective of whom is going to represent you in your real estate transaction.

In this section, I'll explain the difference between an independent brokerage and a franchise, and I'll point out the advantages and disadvantages of both. Remember the following: the brokerage represents the company that your agent works for.

## BARNES & NOBLE VERSUS
## THE INDEPENDENT BOOKSTORE

The difference between an independent real estate company and a franchise is similar to the difference between a large bookstore chain like Barnes & Noble and a small, family-run business. There are several advantages to working with a real estate company that is part of a national network like RE/MAX, Coldwell Banker, Century 21, and more. First of all, they have a large pool of agents working for them.

The bigger offices may have hundreds of realtors working under one broker. These agents will represent many areas. This means that you have your pick of agents with whom you want to work. In addition, because these companies often have offices in other cities, they have large referral networks. For instance, imagine that you are living in Malibu and you want to relocate to Bel Air. Your real estate agent may refer you to an affiliated brokerage that has professionals who specialize in Bel Air.

Next, larger offices also have internal departments with full time legal and marketing staff. With an internal marketing department, they are able to provide their buyers and sellers with many ways to advertise—they can promote their services through the company's Web site, mass mailings, and print ads.

Name recognition is another strength of the franchise real estate companies. People across the nation have heard of companies like Prudential, RE/MAX, and Coldwell Banker, whereas an independent company may only be recognized locally. This branding adds credibility and prestige to the agent and broker of the company.

## BIG COMPANY DISADVANTAGES

The nationally recognized firms work big: Big budgets, big staff, big offices, and big egos. In fact, offices in higher profile areas like Beverly Hills and Malibu are notorious for infighting and the Hollywood celebrity-sized egos of their top producers.

One real estate office is home to three of the most successful agents in Malibu. Together, they sell hundreds of millions of dollars in homes. But this is about all they share in common. Within the real estate community, their distaste for each other is common knowledge. In fact, put them in the same room together and you can almost see the resentment rise in the climate-controlled room.

Furthermore, the large size of these offices translates into high turnover rates among agents and staff members. These companies aggressively recruit people to become real estate agents by offering free training and licensing courses. Through their classes, new agents may have the theoretical knowledge about real estate—in other words, all the information that will help them pass the real estate exam—but they don't have real-world knowledge about the business. Matters like how to represent clients, negotiate deals, and work through difficult situations, are not covered on the board exam.

Therefore, bigger firms may have large numbers of agents working in their offices, which seems impressive, but the inexperience of many of their employees results in negligent behavior that can get them into legal trouble. And the number of court cases that these companies handle every year is growing. Like I mentioned earlier, many of the largest firms decide to settle out of court, which speeds up the process and diminishes attention from the public. Unfortunately, this has also made them targets for people who want to make a quick dollar.

## YOUR PRIVACY COUNTS

In the large brokerages, there are many departments within the company. This means that your personal information will be passed through many hands. In most cases, this is not a threat in terms of identity fraud. But if your goal is to keep your deal under wraps, you are definitely at risk. Think of it this way: Malibu's most high-profile residents chose to live in this city because of its seclusion and exclusivity. Therefore, many buyers want their sales to go completely unnoticed. This is a tough task to accomplish if their transaction is passed from one department's in-box to another and from one part-time office assistant to another. In fact, real estate offices are notorious for spying eyes. I have numerous stories of agents who have looked over one another's faxes and tried to get as much information as possible about their colleague's real estate deals.

I explain the matter of your privacy in greater depth in Chapter 2.

## WATCH OUT FOR HIDDEN FEES, AFFILIATED BUSINESS DISCLOSURE STATEMENTS, AND MORE PAPERWORK

One big firm in Malibu adds a $150 processing fee to any transaction it does. I'm not sure exactly what this covers. Perhaps it's this company's equivalent of the $1.50 surcharge that is added when you use an ATM.

An Affiliated Business Disclosure Statement is a document that notifies you that the company you're working with has ties to mortgage, escrow, title companies, and other businesses relevant to your purchase or sale. This document protects them from liability in the event that a client complains about conflict of interest issues between the real estate brokerage and an affiliated business.

For instance, a real estate company may be affiliated with a title, escrow, or mortgage company. Consider how much it would benefit a parent company if each client also used the company's title, escrow, and mortgage affiliates. Therefore, agents within these brokerages may be encouraged to push the partner companies onto you.

The bigger firms also are notorious for the amount of paperwork they require you to complete. If you've ever bought or sold a home, you know that the legal documents you must sign are immense. In addition to these, the large companies also slip in documents that you may not be aware of—paperwork about which only someone in the legal world would know.

Examples of additional paperwork include disclosures, which are documents that notify all parties about something relevant to the purchase or sale. Often, real estate companies include this paperwork as a result of past lawsuits and as a means to prevent future ones.

If paperwork is something you try to avoid, and you're planning to work with one of the larger companies, be prepared. Regardless of how much you enjoy your current real estate agent, if he works for a big firm, the additional documents are mandatory. I recall receiving an offer from an agent who worked for a nationally recognized brokerage. It was 35 pages. Meanwhile, the same offer in my office is about 16 pages. In this simple transaction, the paperwork from the other brokerage seemed excessive. Imagine the pile of paperwork required for a sale or purchase.

## INFLATED NUMBERS SOUND IMPRESSIVE

"This year, I've sold $200,000,000 in property!" declares Sandra, a top producer. This is certainly a significant amount of money. Or a big real estate agency will state that their agents have sold hundreds of millions of dollars to date. It's time you thought twice about these numbers.

Let's analyze Sandra's sales figure first. Her number comes from the listing prices of the homes she has sold. If she listed a home for $18 million, but it sold for $15 million instead, she'll use the $18 million in her total. Three million here and there can quickly add up. In addition, the amount is a combination of both her listings and ones that she is co-listed with. Co-listing is a way to inflate numbers while having to do very little work selling the property. Typically, one agent is pushing the sale aggressively, and co-listing agents simply have their names underneath the listings. Considering that Sandra may be co-listed in as many as half of her listings, the $200,000,000 figure is considerably less remarkable.

Often sellers request that their agents co-list because they believe that two or three sales people are better than one. The thinking is that in the end, the commission will be split among the agents, so there is nothing for the seller to lose. This may sound favorable, but if your primary agent is an exceptional sales person, co-listing can be a waste of time. The bottom line is that the amount that agents say they have sold usually involves number inflation. All high-profile agents play this game; it's just part of working in Malibu.

Now let's look at the second example. In this case, the brokerage's hundreds of millions of dollars in real estate has more to do with the high number of agents within the company rather than the success of any one real estate agent. In addition, larger firms say that they sell more property than smaller offices, but within any office, only a few agents are responsible for the majority of sales. In fact, in sales, people refer to the 80/20 rule: Eighty percent of sales are handled by 20 percent of staff members, regardless of the company's size.

## SMALLER FIRMS IN MALIBU

Malibu is a tight-knit community, and word gets around quickly. The independent real estate firms that have been in this community for years have reputations that equal those of the larger, nationally recognized companies. Many of these family-owned businesses are the equivalent of the independent bookstores in the Barnes & Noble versus small bookseller analogy I described earlier.

## SMALLER FIRM ADVANTAGES

The independent firms in Malibu specialize in this city. From trailer parks to Carbon Beach, their agents are experts in certain niches or areas. In addition, the number of agents within each brokerage is far less than the numbers in the larger offices. This means that when you break down the sales figures per agent, the independent agents often sell more than their franchise-affiliated counterparts.

Within smaller offices, there are fewer agents than in the large ones, and the agents often have years of experience within Malibu. Many of these agents have built a reputation within this city and have created an extensive network of contacts that will benefit you.

Furthermore, many small-firm agents are specialists in a specific community and may be residents as well. Meanwhile, the national firms recruit large numbers of agents, many of whom may have little knowledge of Malibu.

In fact, buyers often switch their real estate agents after seeing the knowledge and experience of another agent. For example, a colleague tells me the story of how a client dropped his agent to work with her. The client, an actor who had just won an Academy Award, flew his mother from Italy to take a look at the home. The actor, his mother, and his real estate agent met the seller's agent at the La Costa house.

Kathy, the seller's agent, was a big fan of the actor and was excited to meet him. She greeted him at the door and showed him around. The actor was eager to live in Malibu and had many questions. He wanted to know how La Costa compared with other beachfront areas, who else lived in the neighborhood, and what the comparables were for similar homes.

The actor's real estate agent stood in silence as Kathy answered his questions with ease. At one point, the actor asked his agent about the prices La Costa homes have recently sold for. His agent had not researched the area and told him that he would find out later.

Kathy, on the other hand, had sold many homes in La Costa, and she was able to tell him which properties were purchased and how much they sold for. Although Kathy had no intention of eclipsing her colleague, she managed to do so simply by sharing her knowledge with the actor. After the meeting, they all exchanged business cards and parted ways.

In the evening, Kathy was eating dinner with her family at a local restaurant and was sharing about her experience meeting the actor. In the middle of her conversation, her mobile phone rang. It was the actor. He explained that he loved the home in La Costa and wanted her to represent him in the deal. Kathy had to decline the offer because the actor was presently working with another agent. She was a true professional and knew that taking a client from someone else was unethical. He was not satisfied with her answer and was convinced that she could represent him better than his current real estate agent. He would not relent and asked what steps he needed to take to leave his current real estate agent and instead work with her.

Kathy explained that she could only work with him if he were to terminate his working relationship with his current agent. The actor agreed to do this; when he did, the two began looking for homes.

His judgment and persistence paid off. Although he did not purchase the La Costa property, Kathy found him a home elsewhere along the beach. This wasn't the first time she had gained a client by providing information that the other agent did not have. By answering questions better than her competitors, she earned herself another high-profile client.

## LESS PAPERWORK AND FEWER DEPARTMENTS

Smaller firms pass their paperwork along to fewer hands than do the large corporate offices. This makes processing your documents more efficient. In addition, fewer departments mean reduced overhead and costs. You will avoid paying flat, so-called processing fees like the $150 I discussed at the beginning of this chapter.

Furthermore, the reputable independent firms in Malibu are less likely to push title, escrow, and lenders onto their clients. Although agents will recommend companies about which they feel confident, their real estate offices are not owned by or affiliated with them. Therefore, the recommendations will come from experience rather than a desire to fill the pockets of a parent company.

## YOUR PRIVACY

In Malibu, the sale and purchase of real estate often goes completely unnoticed. This is not because of lack of interest from the public. After all, some of the highest profile people in the world have homes here. So, when a supermodel's move into Malibu happens without as much as a whisper, her real estate agent has handled the purchase skillfully. In fact, the most respected agents in Malibu not only build their reputations on their extensive client list but also on their ability to keep a secret.

This is the reason why some of the most famous celebrities in Malibu work with independent real estate agents. In the end, they could care less whether they recognize the company name on the agent's business card. Instead, the real estate agent's reputation for maintaining client confidentiality speaks for itself.

Another reason why independent firms are better at keeping your deal under wraps is that they don't have layers of departments that look over your paperwork. If you consider how many people will see your personal information during your purchase or sale, you can understand how difficult it is to maintain confidentiality. Thus, the fewer eyes that see your personal information, the less likely an information leak will take place.

## INDEPENDENT FIRM DISADVANTAGES

Smaller firms have less real estate agents, less employees, and therefore, smaller budgets. They do not have large marketing departments that the larger companies do. Although they do advertise, they often rely on referrals and word-of-mouth recommendations.

One could argue that the lack of deep pockets of smaller real estate brokerages could put them at greater risk if, say, a huge lawsuit comes along. While it is true that the nation's largest real estate companies have extensive legal departments, the amount of litigation they handle makes this necessary. Meanwhile, at least in Malibu, the prestigious independents have significantly less lawsuits than the larger companies. In fact, some have not ever had someone successfully sue them.

Next, the independent firms do not have national name recognition. Their company name isn't known outside of the community they serve. Thus, if clients would like to move outside of the office's service area, they will have to seek out an unaffiliated real estate brokerage. To remedy this, some independents have created networks with other independent brokerages. But these connections may not be as strong as the ones that exist between brokerages under the same parent company.

## TRUST YOURSELF AND LOOK FOR A GOOD AGENT

When it comes to whom you'll select to represent you in your beach-front property sale or purchase, the decision inevitably involves your emotions. You must trust and feel comfortable with the agent whom you'll work with.

I encourage you to trust your instincts and balance your gut feelings with the information I provided in this chapter. Trusting your emotions is always a good start; after all, you don't want your significant investment in the hands of someone you dislike. But along with feeling a connection to your agent, you must also consider his or her experience, reputation for being an ethical agent, and sales skill. When you combine these two factors—the rapport you have with your agent and his or her credentials—you will avoid many pitfalls and headaches.

# GOOD SELLER'S AGENTS GUARD YOUR PRIVACY

N ot all real estate transactions are the same. From doc stamps to discount points, comparables to confidentiality, the high stakes world of beachfront property requires specialized knowledge that few agents have. This chapter will guide you through the process of finding an agent to meet your needs.

## CAN YOUR AGENT KEEP A SECRET?

Perhaps it's the price of their home or their celebrity status; whatever the reason, many sellers of beachfront property are concerned about the confidentiality of their sale. And in high-profile towns like Malibu, keeping a multi-million dollar deal secret is no easy task. Not only are many steps of the transaction required to be made public, but the sales also often attract unwanted attention. If you aren't convinced, just pick up one of the nationally distributed tabloids describing a celebrity's move into Malibu.

When keeping the deal secret is your goal, your agent must be a purveyor of your privacy. With an agent who has experience selling homes of high-profile owners, exclusive property, or both, you have a good chance of slipping past the public eye. Therefore, an agent who knows the ins and outs of selling beachfront property in areas such as Malibu is your best bet at avoiding unwanted exposure.

For instance, the MLS, or Multiple Listing Service, and a title search are both easy ways for anyone to find out the details of your sale. The MLS is a system that allows brokers to share information about the listings they have for sale. All licensed agents in the United States, who are members of their local board of realtors, have access to the MLS. Having a home listed on the MLS means that agents from all over can see the price for which a home is listed. This is a powerful resource for those buying and selling homes in most of the United States. Unfortunately, if you are selling multi-million dollar beachfront property and want to keep it confidential, the MLS will make your home sale public information.

So how do sellers keep their prices confidential? One way is to not list their property on the MLS. But because all sellers are required to disclose their information on the system, not listing will mean that they must pay a penalty. For most, however, the $250 fine is a small price to pay for the sake of keeping a property unlisted.

## EXPERIENCED AGENTS KNOW HOW TO PROTECT YOUR PRIVACY

Information leaks run rampant in communities like Malibu. People the world over are interested in the lives of its famous residents. Skilled agents who work with high-profile listings, clients, or both, are pros at keeping real estate deals under wraps. On the other hand, inexperienced agents often share information about their high-profile clients to impress others, or they are simply unaware of the level of caution that a secret sale requires. For instance, a water cooler conversation in the office about an agent's celebrity client could result in wide spread news of her client's move into Malibu.

Unfortunately, too many agents are eager to share details about their world-famous clients or their multi-million dollar listings—even if confidentiality agreements have been signed. I've seen it happen time and time again. I've witnessed agents bragging about their celebrity clients or high-profile listings, and I'm quite certain that their clients would be appalled that their information was the topic of office gossip.

Often the lapse in judgment comes from the desire for younger agents to build credibility, while for others they share because they only have a few high-profile listings per year. Experienced agents, however, have built their reputation on their ability to maintain confidentiality no matter what.

## HOW DO AGENTS KEEP A CELEBRITY SALE SECRET?

Malibu is famous for being home to some of the most famous people in the world. But even within Malibu, there are some areas that are more exclusive than others. Take Carbon Beach for example. Also known as "Billionaire's Beach" because of its high number residents with ten-figure incomes, this small cluster of real estate along PCH has some of the most famous residents in all of Malibu. In Carbon, real estate purchases are high-profile news and difficult to keep out of the public eye.

Taylor, a colleague of mine, tells me about the experience she had working with a Hollywood movie producer. Her client was selling his Encinal Bluffs home and wanted to keep it confidential. Both Taylor and the producer had worked together in the past, and he was confident that she would take care of his sale.

The producer was leaving to shoot on location in South Africa. Therefore, he would not be present for the sale. For Taylor, who specialized in multi-million dollar properties, having a client away for part or all of the transaction was common. In this case, the owner told Taylor that he wanted to sell his home for $7 million. He then left the country and put the rest in her hands. Taylor was responsible to find a buyer, sell the home, and keep the entire process secret. This is where experience counts.

Taylor's first task was to find a buyer without advertising the listing on the MLS or in print ads. Someone with a small network would have a difficult time doing this because he wouldn't have a wide-enough range of clients who would be interested in the property.

On the other hand, Taylor used her extensive client base and also networked with her trusted colleagues. These colleagues had clients who were interested in purchasing similar types of property. Furthermore, she knew that her colleagues would keep the entire transaction confidential.

Fortunately for the film producer who was in South Africa, within two weeks Taylor found a buyer for his home. The entire sale—from finding someone to buy the home to closing the deal—happened without as much as a whisper within the community. In the end, the buyer's and seller's agents and the homeowner were the only ones who knew that the listing was for sale, which brings us to the next point: If home prices are not shared with the public, how do homeowners who want to sell similar property find comps—or comparable sales—for properties?

## AN EXTENSIVE LIST OF COMPS SEPARATES SEASONED AGENTS FROM THE REST

Comparables, or comps, are a guide to what the buying public has been willing to pay within the last few months for a similar home in a particular neighborhood. Through these comps, and three other factors, you and your agent determine a suggested selling price for your home. These three additional factors are analyzing market conditions, offering incentives, and estimating your net proceeds. I'll explain these in depth in the next chapter. For now, let's focus on comps.

The Hollywood producer who sold his home without anyone from the community finding out was certainly pleased with the result. Unfortunately, the vow of secrecy required of everyone involved in this transaction made future sales of similar homes in that area more difficult. The reason? One less comparable was available to agents. When you consider that sellers determine the sale price of a home by comparing their home with similar properties on the market, you understand how important comparables are.

The secret sale of one home, which would mean one less comp for everyone else, would not change the face of real estate. But if many homes are not publicly listed, comparables become prized information. And this is where Malibu stands apart from other neighborhoods.

For instance, imagine that a young couple is expecting their first child. For the past five years, their two-bedroom condominium in the Valley has provided them with plenty of space. With a child, however, they now desire a larger home. They phone their agent to see how much their current condominium is worth. Their agent provides them with comparables, or comps, of the prices of condominiums around their neighborhood.

What the agent provided the couple with was an accurate gauge of the value of their home, based on closely related properties. This information was easy to access. In fact, through many web sites, the couple could have found it themselves.

In even more exclusive areas, comparables may be difficult to find—but still not as difficult as in Malibu. Let's take Bel Air as an example. Although the celebrity homeowner status makes sales equally as confidential as in Malibu, other factors come into play. As private as Bel Air is, the homes often share many things in common. For example, they are often 10,000 square feet and located on an acre lot; or a home is 5,000 square feet and located on a 10,000 square foot lot. Therefore, a seller has a wide pool of properties to draw comparables from.

In Malibu, however, there are wide differences between lot sizes and property. A $5 million beach home may have a four-plex of condos to its left and a fifty-year-old fixer-upper on the right. The variation in property and lot sizes, combined with deals that slip past the general public, make comparables a prized resource in Malibu. This is especially true for multi-million dollar homes along the beach.

So how valuable are comparables in Malibu? Here is an example that a colleague shared with me:

A successful businessman wanted to sell his Encinal Bluffs home. Like many successful business people, he left the sale up to his business manager. His manager interviewed several top real estate agents in Malibu and eventually narrowed his search to two. Both agents had impeccable credentials and were well known throughout the real estate community. Both would have done professional work showing the listing and finding potential buyers.

The first agent had solid general knowledge about Malibu. Natalie was a top seller and sold listings throughout the city. If the seller's property were farther inland, she would have had plenty of comps to show the business manager. The downside was that her coastal real estate experience was limited.

Mark, the second agent, was a specialist in Malibu's beachfront real estate. In fact, he had sold more along Malibu's beachfront than any other agent. In addition, many of his listings were never advertised in the community.

Mark and Natalie had impeccable credentials, which resulted in fierce competition. In the end, the decision was in Mark's favor, thanks to an unhappy maid and some exclusive comparables. Let me explain.

Throughout her career, Natalie had worked with many high-profile clients. She had rapport skills that could calm even the most temperamental client. Over the course of the two weeks that she had been working with the seller's business manager, she had visited the home to determine the listing price. One day, Natalie went to the home and Ruby, the maid, was there to let her in. Perhaps Natalie was having a bad day, or perhaps she was in a hurry. Whatever the reason, when Ruby greeted her, Natalie responded by giving her a quick nod and walking past her. The maid was not impressed. Natalie disrespected the wrong person that day.

Two weeks later, the business manager invited Mark to view the property. When he arrived, Ruby warmly greeted him. She was a woman in her mid-40's. The maid took pride in the home and treated it as if it were her own. When she opened the door, Mark introduced himself and presented her with a houseplant. Her sincere thank you and the friendly look on her face reflected an appreciation of his courtesy.

"Would you like me to show you around the house?" she asked.

"Certainly, I'd love to look around," he said.

Ruby knew every detail about the house and was proud to share her knowledge with him. As they were walking to the second floor, Mark thanked her.

"Ruby, I appreciate you showing me the home; you obviously know this place up and down."

"Why, thank you. Gosh, you're so different from the agent who came last week," she said.

"What do you mean?" he asked.

Ruby expressed how unimpressed she was with the first agent. When she greeted Natalie at the door and offered to give her a tour of the home, the agent swiftly declined her offer and viewed the home alone. Mark continued to listen to Ruby explain the details of Natalie's rude behavior.

"I'm really sorry that happened. I'm definitely glad that you were here to help me out. After all, it's obvious that you're like a member of the family," he said.

"You know, when I was younger, I prayed to God that someone rich would take care of me—you know, like a knight in shining armor," she said.

"And did that happen?" he asked.

"Well, sort of. I work for a rich family, so I guess they take care of me…It wasn't quite what I expected. But you know what they say, 'Be careful what you wish for.'"

They both shared a laugh. Ruby and Mark continued to have a pleasant conversation. Ruby explained that she looked after the owner, who was retired, seven days per week. This was his beach home; his primary residence was in Beverly Hills. He decided to sell because he believed that the market was at its peak. Ruby also shared about her own family, her children, and her husband who had passed away ten years ago.

Mark's sincerity and interest in Ruby's life earned her trust. He also realized that Ruby's disdain for the other agent meant that she was willing to share more about the transaction itself. Fortunately, it was clear to him that Ruby had a mission: Make the first agent lose the deal at all cost.

"So tell me Ruby, who was this other agent that came here last week?" Mark asked.

"Ugh. That woman. She was so rude! To think, I was trying to help her and she treated me like I was a nobody!" she said.

"Do you remember her name?" he asked.

"Yes her name, it was Nancy… No, it was Nat…Natalie. Yes, it was Natalie."

"If it's the same person I'm thinking of, I know her well—about my height, brown hair and eyes, right?" he asked.

"Yes, that's it. In fact, I still have her business card. She handed it to me on her way out. Do you want to see it?" she asked.

"Yes, if you don't mind," he said.

"Of course not. I'm surprised I didn't tear it up and throw it away. To think, 24 years with this family, and she just walked in and acted like I was nothing," she said.

Ruby went to a drawer, fumbled through some papers, and pulled out Natalie's business card. Her photo was on it, and the card read, "Malibu's Top Producer."

In high stakes real estate, knowing your competition is often a mystery shrouded in guesses and uncertainty. You know whom you may be up against, because the circle of top producers is small, but you're often unsure exactly who is competing with you. For Ruby to reveal Natalie's name to Mark was the equivalent of a stockbroker knowing the name of a privately held company that is about to go public.

"Listen, Ruby, I don't mean to pry, but were you the only one here when Natalie arrived?" he asked.

"Yes...Well, sort of, she was on her cell phone talking to someone almost the whole time," she responded.

"Hmmm...then she probably didn't have a lot of time to talk to you," he said.

"No, she just talked and talked away on her phone. After a while, I just acted like she wasn't there. And you know what?" she asked.

"Yes?" he asked.

"She told the person on the phone that she thought the house could sell for $9 million," she said.

Recall the example that I used earlier, when I compared discovering a competing agent's name with a financial planner knowing the name of a company that will soon go public. Well, now the financial investor not only knows the name of the business that will go public, but he also knows the stock's initial selling price. This significant twist of events gave Mark the information he needed to gain an upper hand in the bid.

When he heard Natalie's suggested listing price, he knew the next steps that he needed to take. Mark pulled together comps that he had acquired over the past few months—comparables that only he had. He did a thorough analysis of the area. He presented the results of his research and the comparables to the client. While the first agent, Natalie, determined the value of the home at $9 million, she had little solid information to support her offer. He, on the other hand, had comps that allowed him to justify a price of $9.5 million, or $500,000 more than Natalie's suggested price. After considering the two agents, the business manager hired Mark. The comparables were certainly a deciding factor. Mark placed the home on the MLS. Once it was listed, the agent received a phone call from Natalie.

"Hey Mark, I see you got a great listing today," she said.

"Which one?" he asked.

"The house on Encinal Bluffs. If you don't mind, could you tell me how you got it?" Natalie asked, acting as if she knew nothing about the property—let alone the maid.

"Well, I got a good tip, and the rest was pretty easy. The sellers were ready to move fast. Why do you ask?"

"Just curious...Congratulations," she said.

Unfortunately for Natalie, her disregard for the maid was a bad business move. In Malibu and exclusive areas everywhere, maids, gardeners, and maintenance staff work within the private circle of homes and are sometimes just like members of the family. Therefore, they are often the best source of information if someone from the outside wants to know about events within the home. The power they yield within a household should never be overlooked. Ruby was no exception. In fact, she had been with the family for 24 years. She not only had access to the decision makers within the family, but she also garnered a great deal of respect after years of committed service.

Whether it's the owner of a multi-million dollar home, her business manager, her maid, or her dog walker, a real estate agent must treat everyone with respect. To the bottom-line-driven agent, a person like Ruby may seem like an outsider in the transaction and therefore someone who doesn't deserve to be treated well. In the end, she knew more details than anyone else and was willing to share her information with anyone who wanted to listen. The next chapter will give you specific questions to ask when selecting a real estate agent to sell your home.

# FINDING THE BEST SELLER'S AGENT

*Nine Important Questions to Ask*

R eal estate agents are all over the place. And when the market is hot, agents seem to slither out of nowhere like snails after a spring rain. So how do you pick the right one? In this chapter, I'll take you through the steps to find an agent who will get you the highest price on your investment, keep you out of legal battles, and sell your home as quickly as possible.

The best agents, the ones who have years of career experience and still work hard today, get most of their business from past clients and referrals. Generating business this way is certainly well deserved. At the same time, as a seller you should make sure that the agent, who represented you or your friend five years ago, is still working at the top of her game. Therefore, regardless of the agent's reputation, it is in your best interest to continue to ask the right questions and keep your eye out for other agents.

When you're looking for an agent to represent you in your beach-front sale, be certain to ask the following questions:

1. Are his or her comparables up-to-date? And if you own an exclusive home, does the agent have comps no one else knows?
2. How many beachfront properties has the agent sold, and does he or she have a list of satisfied clients?
3. Does the agent limit the number of concurrent listings he or she will accept?
4. How does the agent plan to represent your home?
5. How much time can the agent commit to your sale?
6. Has the agent been involved in any lawsuits?
7. How will the agent analyze market conditions?
8. If necessary, does the agent suggest that you offer incentives?
9. Can the agent estimate your net proceeds?

## 1. ARE HIS OR HER COMPARABLES UP-TO-DATE?

Like I described in the previous chapter, comparables are a beachfront real estate agent's best-kept secret. While the average agent may know about a couple of sales in an exclusive area, the experienced agent will have a comprehensive list of comps for the same location. This is especially true if you are listing a home in an area where deals are often confidential. For example, imagine if two agents are competing for a beachfront listing. Agent 1 may suggest that the house should sell for $5.8 million, while Agent 2 will say $6 million. A seller may initially believe that $6 million is a better price. But if the $5.8 million price was based on a comparable that only Agent 1 had, that agent's recommendation may be more accurate.

In addition, make sure that your agent is well connected. It's through connections that he will be able to meet the individual needs of your beachfront property. His network of colleagues will give him access to comparables and buyers, as well as referrals to reliable inspectors, title, and escrow providers. The connections that he has built over the years are a significant part of what will help your sale go smoothly.

## 2. HOW MANY BEACHFRONT HOMES HAS THE AGENT SOLD, AND DOES HE OR SHE HAVE A LIST OF SATISFIED CLIENTS?

In high-profile areas like Malibu, agents spend thousands, and often tens of thousands of dollars per year on marketing themselves. Slick marketing and fancy websites are effective ways to create name recognition, but as a consumer, you must look beyond what appears in print and online.

You may be motivated to work with a highly qualified agent who has been in the business for a long time. But if you are looking to sell in Carbon Beach, The Colony, or Encinal Bluffs, and the agent has no experience in these areas, consider looking for someone else. Even if he has sold multi-million dollar homes throughout his career, you want to work with a beachfront specialist. This is because beachfront real estate has many aspects that require specialized knowledge.

For example, I know an agent who specializes in mobile homes. In fact, he holds 90 percent of the market in his area. In other words, nine out of ten people who buy or sell a mobile home work with him. He knows this segment of real estate better than anyone else. Therefore, if you wanted to buy or sell your mobile home, he would be the most qualified person.

Similarly, selling along Malibu's beachfront is unlike selling anywhere else in the city. The more the agent knows about the almost 20 communities along PCH, the types of homes in each, its sales trends, as well as technical matters such as building codes, the better off your home sale will be.

Also, request to see referrals, a partial list of clients, and copies of any editorial coverage (such as *The Los Angeles Times*) that the agent's listings have received. When you ask to see these references, make sure that they are up-to-date. An article from *The Times* that appeared ten years ago is impressive, but not as much as an agent who has a "Home of the Week" article several times per year.

### 3. DOES THE AGENT LIMIT THE NUMBER OF CONCURRENT LISTINGS HE OR SHE WILL ACCEPT?

A colleague shared with me a story about a real estate agent who works in another city. The agent, Tina, promotes herself as "The Number 1 Producer." She certainly works hard and sells many homes. In fact, at times she will have 25 listings. This sounds impressive—and it is. But taking on so many listings at once diminishes the quality of her work. She has the high numbers and effective marketing. For instance, her print ads say, "I've sold $195 million in homes this year!" But her focus on volume decreases the time she can spend working with each client. So what does she do? She has a staff of assistants and co-lists, which boosts her sales figures with little work on her part. Furthermore, she focuses on certain high-profile listings at the expense of others. In fact, many who interview her as potential listing agent complain that Tina is more interested in building her image than selling their home.

Think of homes like children. Each one has a completely different personality, and each one will attract a different type of person. A parent with 25 children cannot possibly give each child the same amount of attention each day. For example, when Charles, son Number 22, gets out his cell phone and calls his father to ask, "Daddy, can you pick me up from surf practice?" His father will most likely have to answer with, "I'm sorry, which child are you?" After all, a father will have enough difficulty remembering all of his children's names—let alone their daily schedules, birthdays, food allergies, and tastes in music.

Similarly, an agent who has 25 listings cannot commit the time needed to quickly sell your home. This agent will inevitably have to select which homes to focus more attention on. He won't return calls quickly; and he may not know the details of your home the way you would like him to.

In the example of Tina, the attention she gives to each listing is stretched thin. Her assistants do their part, but if you're expecting that she will be able to make it on time to every appointment, know the details of your extensive remodel, and open every window you specify during a showing, chances are that you will be disappointed. In fact, because of her busy schedule, she is consistently late to showings.

In the next section, I'll explain why it is critical that the agent show up at the property before the appointment time. For now, I suggest that you work with an agent who carries no more than ten homes at once. Any more, and she won't be able to give your home the attention it needs to attract the best buyers.

## 4. HOW DOES THE AGENT PLAN TO REPRESENT YOUR HOME?

Malibu residents have a reputation for being a hardy lot. They brave the damaging effects of salty air on their homes, the twists and turns of PCH, floods, and the occasional mudslide, all of which are a small sacrifice to live in one of the most exclusive areas in the world. Therefore, when an agent sells beachfront property, the lifestyle he promotes is just as important as the home itself. In your sale, your goal is that your agent shows your home in all its upgraded, renovated, or "for-sale-as-is" glory. Your agent should know the most important details of your house, which means that he has researched your home and has asked you detailed questions about it.

Let us return to our example of the busy agent, Tina. Her workload of 25 homes means that she has to focus on the hottest listing while neglecting others. On the other hand, an agent who limits her number of concurrent listings is able to invest the time necessary to create an effective marketing strategy. During a showing, she knows precise details about your home so she can answer questions as they arise, without the excuse of, "Let me get back with you about that." She will arrive early to the listing appointment and present it exactly to your specifications, meaning if you want candles burning and Mozart's Hunt Quartet playing through your home's sound system, she'll make sure these things happen every time. This attention to detail is especially important for multi-million dollar listings. Owners of these homes may request that the fireplace be lit, a newspaper be put on patio furniture, and a breakfast setting be placed in the master suite. The sellers know that these visual cues will entice buyers.

An agent who is committed to selling your property will arrive ahead of the appointment time to make your home as inviting as possible. This is crucial when your home has several features that require prior preparation, or when a last minute need must be taken care of. For example, the high winds from the night before may have littered the driveway with road debris and leaves. The well-prepared agent will have time to quickly sweep the entrance before the buyer arrives. In addition, there will be a parking space saved for the client—and along most of PCH, parking can be very difficult to find.

Once the buyer approaches the property and opens the door, the listing agent will be ready to greet him instead of arriving alongside him and opening up a dark home. For an agent like top-producing Tina, the buyer stands in the unlit entrance as Tina sets up the home, which means that important matters may be overlooked. Unfortunately, if prospective buyers must wait and watch as the agent sets up, the all-important first impression is compromised.

Upon the buyer's arrival, the agent will greet the client and immediately create rapport with him. The agent realizes that she will set the tone for the showing. Her personality will be warm and friendly, and her goal will be to make the client feel comfortable. After all, the buyers are strangers to the home. Just as an effective host will immediately make guests feel like they can make themselves at home, an experienced agent knows how to make a client feel comfortable during a showing. Unfortunately, many agents are awkward and have poor communication skills. This will make the buyers uneasy as they walk into what is possibly their future home. This will limit their ability to enjoy the experience.

On the other hand, sometimes people can feel too comfortable when they see a home. A colleague told me about her experience showing a home to a famous Hollywood actress. She recently had won an Academy Award and earned accolades for her stunning Oscar-night appearance. The actress was looking at a listing along Malibu's exclusive Carbon Beach. Before she arrived, the agent's assistant had thoroughly prepared the home, which included opening the windows and patio doors, turning on lights, and setting up the furniture on the deck.

At the appointment time, the actress arrived, accompanied by her four small dogs. Like the trend in Hollywood these days, she brought her entourage of diminutive dogs with her. Once she entered the home, she released her grip and proudly watched as her pets scrambled away—claws scraping the tile floors. She and the agent walked throughout the home, and he pointed out its key features: the view from the master bedroom, the tile floors (that were being clawed by the pets), and the upgraded kitchen. As he pointed to the impressive ocean view, he noticed that one dog was calmly sitting on the deck.

When the actress and the agent made their way to the patio, the dog quickly scampered back inside. Meanwhile, the two stood watching the ocean view. The agent shared about the beauty of beachfront living and the high-profile neighbors that lived next door. It was a clear Malibu day, and the agent looked down to rest his eyes from the seawater's glare. He suddenly noticed a brown mass baking on a sun-bleached plank of the deck. As he lowered his head slightly more, he saw that the shapeless pile was flattened by a paw print.

He turned and looked inside and noticed the dog sitting on the white couch. When the agent and the actress entered the house, brown paw prints revealed the path the dog took to make his way to his resting place. He seemed to be relaxing to the sound of waves, taking a well-deserved break after relieving himself outside.

The actress walked up to her dog and stroked its head, ignoring the already-eaten designer dog food that dotted the custom floors. The agent was appalled yet uncertain how to react. If he pointed out the dog's misdeed, he could risk offending the actress. At the same time, he wanted the client to take responsibility for her pups. Meanwhile, he maintained calm and acted as if nothing had happened. The actress then asked if he would watch her dogs so she could take a walk on the sand. He obliged, and as she stepped out onto the beachfront, the agent phoned his boss.

"Kim, you won't believe what just happened," he said. He explained what the dog had done. He continued, "And I can't believe that she saw it and didn't do anything. I'm so ticked off right now. You've got to come by and help me."

They finished their conversation. Kim immediately left her office and made her way down PCH. Within minutes she arrived at the home. She entered with a roll of paper towels under her arm, saw the two talking on the deck, walked toward them, dropped the paper towels on the couch, then seamlessly entered the conversation. "Isn't this a beautiful house? And what a view!" she said to the actress as the three looked out onto the Pacific Ocean.

"Hey Kim, when did you get here? Yes, I love this house," the actress responded.

The three had a lively conversation then walked back into the living room. Kim casually glanced on the floor. "Oh my, look what we have here," she said as she tore a square from the roll of paper towels. She then got down on her knees and started wiping the brown paw prints off the floor.

"Why, let me help you with that," the actress said as she lowered herself toward the floor to help. "I'm so sorry. Did my dogs do this?" she asked.

"Who knows—it's a small price to pay for such cute dogs," Kim said.

As the two cleaned up the mess, Kim's assistant stood and watched, amazed at how Kim had managed the situation so well. He slipped away back to the office just as quickly as Kim entered the home, relieved that she was ready to take over. More importantly, for him, he was satisfied that the actress took responsibility for her dog's lack of open house etiquette.

Kim had effectively handled a difficult situation. Another agent may have unskillfully confronted the client or ignored what had happened. She, however, was able to compel the client to help clean up the mess while avoiding alienating her. An agent with years of experience working under countless circumstances like these will go a long way in making your home sale go smoothly.

## 5. HOW MUCH TIME CAN THE AGENT COMMIT TO YOUR SALE?

Whether your home is a 700 square foot condominium or a three-lot wide beachfront estate, investing time is critical to selling your home. Even if your home isn't going to make the "Home of the Week" section of the *LA Times*, your agent needs to commit to getting your listing sold.

An agent who is overloaded will most likely spend less time on homes that aren't as prestigious as his other listings. As any agent will tell you, showing a listing at its best takes a tremendous amount of experience and work. Before a buyer even steps foot in the property, preparing the advertising is often just as time consuming as showing it. For instance, to get a home featured in a popular real estate magazine, the agent must arrange and show up for the photo shoot, prepare copy for the print ads, select the best photos, and review the final layout. If a client wants to have the home photographed during different times of the day, the process will take even longer.

I had a client who, after all the ads were ready to go to press, requested that the photos be re-taken; he had purchased a new lamp and wanted it to appear in the advertisements. In other instances, a client may want his property to be shot once at sunset and again at midday, or he will request that the pictures be taken at certain angles and highlight specific features of the home. The point is that all of this will take time on the part of the agent.

For the higher-end properties, DVD's add another level of high-impact marketing. A DVD is something that a buyer can take home and watch at her convenience. The presentations typically run for five minutes. Within that time, the main features of the home will appear, and the home can be shown as it appears throughout the day. For instance, a spectacular ocean view can be shot in the morning, afternoon, and evening. DVD's can be distributed to buyers when they attend a showing or mailed out to people who have seen the listing advertised elsewhere.

## 6. HAS THE AGENT BEEN INVOLVED IN ANY LAWSUITS?

Across all aspects of society today, from automobile accidents to over-heated lattés at the local coffee house, litigation is running rampant. In real estate, agents, brokerages, and homeowners are being sued at record numbers for inaccurate disclosure statements and misrepresented listings. Mistakes are sometimes unintentional and may have more to do with inexperience or sloppiness than outright fraud. But whether it's because your agent is cutting corners to close a sale quickly or because he is dishonest, working with agents like these put you at risk for litigation. To avoid this, select an agent who comes highly recommended and has impeccable credentials.

## REAL ESTATE TRANSFER DISCLOSURE STATEMENTS AND MISREPRESENTED LISTINGS

In every real estate sale in California, sellers complete a Real Estate Transfer Disclosure Statement. This is a checklist that explains all known defects of the property. Agents and sellers put themselves at legal risk when they fail to disclose all known problems about the property in this statement. If an agent, seller, or both deliberately hide defects, they are opening themselves up to possible legal battles. Problem areas could include things like mold, doors that don't open, dry rot, or peeling paint.

On the other had, agents who are diligent record keepers not only ask the owner questions about the house, perform a detailed walk-through and include their observations in the Transfer Disclosure Statement, they may also take photos or record the walk-through on camera. A walk-through means that an agent will look at the home, one room at a time, and take notes about what he sees. He may notice mold, cracks in the walls, or dry rot underneath a door. Although the walk-through is not a substitute for a building inspection, it is an important step that allows the agent to represent the property honestly.

A warning to the seller: If you know about a defective part of the home and neglect to tell your agent about it, and the buyer finds out later, you will be liable. Therefore, you must tell your agent about anything that is amiss.

Agents who misrepresent listings also leave themselves open to lawsuits. For instance, a buyer puts in an offer and the selling agent tells her, "There's an offer for $50,000 more than yours, but I'll give it to you for $60,000." In reality, there is no other offer. This is called misrepresentation and is a violation of the law.

Some agents get themselves into trouble because they take money from title, mortgage, or inspection companies. An agent will tell his client that he has good contacts with a home inspector and will only refer one inspector to him instead of three. The inspector, in turn, gives the agent $50 every time he sends him a client. On the other hand, if an agent has a home inspector who has a reputation for good work, then the correct approach to refer the inspector to the buyer is, "I know a highly qualified inspector, but here are two others to give you an unbiased recommendation."

## BIG FIRMS THAT SETTLE OUT OF COURT OPEN THEMSELVES UP FOR EVEN MORE LEGAL HEADACHES

Even if the agent hasn't been involved in a lawsuit, if his brokerage has, you may be a target for a court battle. This is because when the big firms are sued, they often decide to settle without trial. In many instances, their reasoning is that avoiding a potentially long legal battle will save money, time, and negative exposure from the media. Unfortunately, the high number of out-of-court settlements for even frivolous lawsuits has set a bad precedent. Many unscrupulous plaintiffs have filed lawsuits against these big firms because they know that they have a chance to get a settlement without going to trial, regardless of how groundless their accusations may be.

So how do you know if an agent or the brokerage has been involved in a lawsuit? First, ask the agent. If you are not satisfied with his or her answer, ask other agents. The real estate community is small, and bad news spreads quickly.

## 7. HOW WILL THE AGENT ANALYZE
## MARKET CONDITIONS?

Market conditions can change not only from city to city but from block to block. With almost 20 communities along PCH, this is especially true in Malibu's beachfront. Therefore, your agent's understanding of the different features of each area along Malibu's coast is what makes her the expert. She should be able to tell you the frequency of home sales in your area. For instance, when the market is booming, sales can happen within days. But when times are slower, sales can take months or even years. In a seller's market, buyers may pay more than your listing price; in a buyers market, you may have to sell for less.

In the case of multi-million dollar beachfront properties, your agent should take the market analysis one step further. Once she gives you comps, she should do a market test to determine if buyers are willing to pay the potential listing price. A market test may involve showing your property to the public, discussing it with colleagues, or going through her list of clients to see if any of them are interested in your home. These clients include the homebuyers themselves, their lawyers, or their business managers. In the event that you want to keep the transaction confidential, the agent must rely on her contacts.

As a homeowner, you certainly want to get the highest price possible within reason. Fortunately, one of the advantages of beachfront property is that it pulls powerfully at people's emotions. Listings can sell for far higher than market value because a buyer desires to live by the beach and is willing to pay top dollar.

## 8. IF NECESSARY, DOES THE AGENT SUGGEST THAT YOU OFFER INCENTIVES?

The marketing plan you create to sell your home depends on your needs and your personality. Some sellers either have to sell in a hurry or hate the idea of bargaining, so they immediately list their home at the lowest price possible. Others sell their homes higher than what the market dictates because they are able to wait or want to see if anyone is willing to purchase their home for top dollar.

However you decide to sell, it is difficult to know how prospective buyers will respond. Within a few days, your home may generate so much interest that a bidding war ensues. Or after three weeks, you may have no buyers at all so you decide it's time to lower your price. In either case, it's always a good idea to plan your tactic ahead of time. This will prevent emotion from getting in the way of wise financial judgment. A plan of action, written in advance, is a way of maintaining peace of mind when things don't go as planned.

For instance, cash incentives are one way to bring in buyers. These are especially attractive to buyers who are "cash poor"—in other words, they don't have assets that are liquid. Often cash incentives are as effective as lowering your list price. Incentives include offering to pay the following:

- Some or all of the buyer's closing costs
- Discount points required by the buyer's lender
- Bonus points for the selling broker

The last point means that you will give your agent a monetary bonus (in addition to her commission) if she sells your property by a certain date. Bonuses are effective if you have to sell in a hurry, or if your property is not generating as much interest from buyers as you had anticipated. An example of this is if you solicited a real estate agent in a newspaper. The ad would read, "Bonus for the agent who brings in a successful offer by December."

## 9. CAN THE AGENT ESTIMATE YOUR NET PROCEEDS?

Your agent has given you comparables and has tested the market, and you have decided your plan of action to sell your home. Now it's time to calculate how much cash you earn once your sale is complete. This is especially important as you start looking for another home to buy.

You determine your profits by subtracting the following from your estimated sales price:

1. Payoff figure on your present loan(s)
2. Agent commission
3. Any prepayment penalty on your mortgage
4. Attorney's fees, if you have any
5. Unpaid property taxes

In addition, depending on the specific requirements of your listing, you or the buyer may be expected to pay the following:

1. Title insurance premium
2. Transfer taxes
3. Survey fees
4. Structural pest control inspection report and repairs

5. Recording fees
6. Homeowner association transfer fees and document preparation
7. Home protection plan
8. Natural hazard disclosure report

In this chapter, I've given you a guideline of qualities to look for when you are finding an agent to represent you. Taking time to evaluate your current or prospective seller's agent will pay off in the end. Doing so will help you earn top dollar for your home, keep yourself out of legal problems, and sell your home faster.

For review, here are nine questions to consider asking when looking for a seller's agent:

1. Are his or her comparables up-to-date? And if you own an exclusive home, does the agent have comps that no one else knows about?
2. How many beachfront properties has the agent sold, and does he or she have a list of satisfied clients?
3. Does the agent limit the number of concurrent listings he or she will accept?
4. How does the agent plan to represent your home?
5. How much time can the agent commit to the sale?
6. Has the agent been involved in any lawsuits?
7. How will the agent analyze market conditions?
8. If necessary, does the agent suggest that you offer incentives?
9. Can the agent estimate your net proceeds?

Follow these steps, and you'll have an agent who will take good care of your sale and make your beachfront property well worth the investment. In the next chapter, we'll explore the buying side of real estate.

# A BEACHFRONT SPECIALIST CAN MAKE YOU MILLIONS

Allow me to begin this chapter with an analogy. When clients need someone to repair their septic system, I refer them to a specialist. This is because septic systems are complex, and repairs require specific knowledge. Similarly, when you're looking to buy along Malibu's beachfront, an agent who specializes in beachfront has insider information that can potentially save you an immense amount of time and money. Trust in your agent will make the difference between buying your dream home and settling for something less.

In this chapter, you'll read about tax-deferred exchanges and multiple offers. I'll describe what separates skilled professionals from their less experienced counterparts. Next, I'll give you an example of how one agent made his client millions from a tax-deferred exchange.

## WHEN TRAILER PARK MILLIONAIRES SELL THEIR HOMES

A couple who made their fortune from trailer park homes wanted to sell their Broad Beach residence. They contacted their agent and arranged for her to look at the house. When Kathleen arrived, she noticed a disagreeable doublewide-decorating theme. She was certain that this would dissuade potential buyers but said nothing to her clients.

Kathleen's first complaint was that the exterior of the home was surrounded by artificial ivy, sun-bleached to a lime green. Next, she thought that the clay pots that held the plants were a feeble attempt to convince visitors that the greenery came from Mother Nature, rather than from a factory in Southeast Asia. Inside, the silk plant theme continued. In addition, there were decaled angels stuck to the ceiling.

In Kathleen's eyes, the exterior overgrowth was more silk weed than silk plant, and from the beginning she intended to get rid of it. To her satisfaction, the owners recently moved out of the home, which gave her the freedom to make cosmetic adjustments without them finding out.

Meanwhile, an actor who had recently won an Academy Award for his role in a sleeper hit was looking to buy a home along Malibu's beachfront. His agent saw the Broad Beach home on the MLS (Multiple Listing Service) and arranged for a showing. Kathleen, the seller's agent, arrived ahead of the appointment and began to clear the polyester foliage with slash-and-burn intensity. Within minutes, she broke the clay pots, left the shards in the outdoor fireplace, ripped the silk overgrowth off of the walls, and unraveled the faux vines that surrounded the entrance. Inside, she couldn't mask the angels on the ceiling, but she managed to hide the plastic plants that dotted the living room.

By the appointment time, Kathleen was satisfied with her work. When the actor arrived, he walked through the home and immediately fell in love with it. Afterwards, his real estate agent advised the actor to put in an offer at full price. Furthermore, he suggested that the actor submit the offer right away. Otherwise, the property could go into a multiple offer situation. His client agreed. Kathleen was delighted to share the news with her trailer park clients.

What happened here makes two important points. First, the trailer park owner's real estate agent went above and beyond what her clients expected. She realized that getting rid of the fake ivy outside would make the house much more appealing. Perhaps all agents won't go to these lengths, even the best ones. But what is important is that good agents will go to great lengths to get the job done.

Second, the actor's real estate agent made a suggestion that at first seemed foolish. Why, for instance, did the actor agree with his real estate agent's recommendation to offer at full price? After all, wouldn't he save money by offering to buy the home for less than the listing price? In this case, the agent knew that the house would sell quickly, and he wanted to avoid competing for the purchase.

## MAKE SURE THAT YOUR AGENT IS A BEACHFRONT SPECIALIST

Whether you're living in the city or by the beach, working with an experienced agent means that she knows the area where you plan to buy. She will know about market conditions within her area and will make recommendations to get your offer accepted by a seller.

The miles of shoreline that weave along PCH make Malibu a destination known the world over. What most people don't know is that this stretch through Malibu has some of the most diverse costal property in California. Each beach has its own qualities that appeal to its residents for different reasons. For instance, Malibu Cove Colony attracts those who want beachfront property away from PCH, whereas La Costa Beach residents often like that it's closer to the Westside of Los Angeles.

Therefore, Malibu's beachfront requires specific knowledge. Even within a couple of miles, the characteristics between one property and another can change dramatically. For example, the difference between dry beach and wet beach or the difference between the almost 20 communities along Malibu's shore are key factors when you are deciding where to live.

When you're looking to buy beachfront property, an agent who knows the area will direct you to listings that will fit your needs. In addition, she will find the best location and property based on the amount you would like to spend. If you are uncertain of what type of property you want, an experienced agent will listen to you and give you relevant suggestions. If, however, you are sure where you would like to live in Malibu, an experienced agent will use her contacts to find you a property in the area of your choice.

## MULTIPLE OFFERS AND TAX DEFERRED EXCHANGES

Whether you're looking to buy a condo in Las Flores or a one acre estate in Pointe Dume Bluffs, a knowledgeable agent will have the connections and information that will save you time and money. A professional who has successfully represented buyers for years will know facts about the market before everyone else. She will have many leads and will know how to negotiate aggressively on your behalf.

The last point is of great importance when you are competing for a listing that has multiple offers. A multiple offer is when a home is listed for sale and more than two potential buyers submit an offer. The most experienced real estate agents pride themselves on their ability to win a listing in a multiple offer setting. In these competitive situations, with millions of dollars at stake, an agent's quick thinking and aggressive negotiation skills are put to the test. Here is an example:

A few years ago, Olivia was looking for a home that was located in The Colony. She wanted a beach house that she could use as an investment property. Her plan was to buy a home and rent it out for about $20,000 a month. At the time, Olivia lived in Cleveland, Ohio. She phoned the Malibu agent that she had been working with for years. Max, the agent, quickly found her a $2 million home; she purchased it, then rented it out. Two years later, she sold the property for $5 million—earning $3 million from her investment. At this point, she knew that unless she filed a 1031 tax-deferred exchange and purchased another property right away, she would owe capital gains tax on her profit.

Generally, gains are subject to income tax in the year in which they occur. In some cases, the IRS will allow the recognition of capital gains to be deferred into the future through a 1031 tax-deferred exchange.

What is a 1031 tax-deferred exchange? As defined in section 1031 of the Internal Revenue Code, it's when an investor disposes of her income-producing property and uses all of her equity to trade for another investment property. When an investor executes an exchange and trades all of the equity, the investor defers all capital gains. Taxes are deferred so long as the taxpayer does not receive either of the following:

1. Mortgage relief
2. Boot, which is unlike kind property such as cash, a yacht, jewelry, or anything that is not real property.

The investor cannot receive cash, other additional consideration, or boot because this will result in reportable gain for tax purposes in the amount of boot received.

Occasionally, a property is simultaneously exchanged for another, so most likely, a delayed exchange has to take place. In the case of a delayed exchange (i.e., a non-simultaneous exchange), the property is sold with the proceeds held by a third party until a new property is identified within 45 days and escrow is closed within 180 days.

In Olivia's case, with $3 million dollars to spend and time running out before having to pay taxes on it, she phoned Max from her Cleveland office and asked him to find her another beachfront home. After doing some research, he phoned her back.

"Olivia, there's a listing in The Colony that just came up," he said.

"Tell me about it," she said.

"It's great—three stories with two master suites—right on the beach. The selling agent is a good friend of mine—really professional."

"How much?"

"They're asking $5.9 million. It's really what you've been looking for. It does need some work, though. But then it'll be ready to lease right away."

"Like what?" she asked.

"Some upgrades. But to get the most out of it, it'll take more work," he said.

"I trust you. If you think it's worth buying, I'd love to come and take a look at it."

"The only problem is, as you know, the market is pretty hot in Malibu. By the time you got here, it might be sold already."

"You're right." She pauses for a moment and says, "Time's running out for me to buy another house. If you think it's a good deal, let's put in an offer. Just add a contingency about the inspection."

Like many homeowners along Malibu's beachfront, Olivia was a savvy businessperson. Although she wouldn't be able to see the listing herself, she wanted to make sure that if the property inspection had negative remarks on it, she would still be able to back out of the deal.

"That's what I like to hear; I knew that you wouldn't waste any time on this," he said.

"And you know that once I see the house, I'd better like it. Otherwise, the inspection had better go badly," she said.

Max was used to her no-nonsense personality and took the light-hearted threat as a sign of her trust in him. They agreed to the terms of the offer. He went to work to draft the contract.

He drafted and submitted Olivia's offer of $5 million— $900,000 less than the listing price. Soon after, the seller sent a counter offer. At that point, the selling agent told Max that there were multiple offers on the home. In a situation like this, where buyers are competing for a listing, the buyer's agent must act decisively. Max realized that having more than one potential buyer meant that the seller had an advantage. To make matters more complicated, he was uncertain about the terms of the competing agent's offer.

It was Wednesday when Max received the counter offer. The seller came down only a little from the original price. His terms were that the price of the home was $5.5 million with a thirty-day escrow. Max had until 5:00 p.m. on Friday to respond. Fortunately, he was well connected in the Malibu real estate community. In fact, the seller's agent was one of his close colleagues. Without breaking the rules of confidentiality, the seller's agent let Max know that the competing buyer had requested to see the property again and wanted to do this before submitting the second offer.

On Thursday, Max's assistant was driving in The Colony to look at another home. At 2:00 p.m., as he was returning to the office, he drove past the home that Olivia was planning to buy. He noticed a car parked in front. When he drove in for a closer look, he saw an agent walking inside.

He immediately picked up his cell phone and called Max.

"Hey Max, I have some news for you," he said.

"What is it?" he asked.

"I'm in The Colony now, and I drove by the house Olivia wants to buy."

"Yeah, I'm still thinking about how we're going to get it for her."

"Well, the other agent's car is in front of the house, and I just saw him walk in. I think he's there for the second showing."

"Great news; that's exactly what I needed to hear," Max said.

Max then phoned Olivia. He explained that the competing buyer wanted to see the house again. Then he let her know that she had to submit a counter offer by 5:00 p.m. the next day.

He gave her the details of his plan. Olivia authorized Max to submit a final offer. The terms were as follows: $5.2 million for the home, all cash, and a 30-day escrow. The critical piece of the offer stated that it would expire by 5:00 p.m. that day. Thus, as the competing agent was looking at the home for a second time, believing that he had until 5:00 p.m. the next day to accept or counter the offer, Max sent the seller an offer to which he had to respond within hours.

Max put the seller in a difficult situation. If he accepted Max's offer, the deal would be done. If he were to reject it, the seller would have to wait until 5:00 p.m. the next day for the competing agent to respond. By waiting, the seller risked receiving an offer that wasn't as clean as

Max's. Perhaps the other buyer would place additional contingencies in the offer, or perhaps the price he offered was going to be less than what Olivia would pay.

Max's plan gave Olivia an advantage over both the competing buyer and the seller. When the seller's agent returned from showing the home to the other buyer, Max's offer was waiting on her desk. With only a couple of hours to respond, she immediately contacted her client and discussed the terms with him.

At 5:00 p.m. that day, the seller accepted Olivia's bid. The homeowner would have certainly preferred to receive the counter offer by Friday so he would have time to consider offers from two buyers. But Max was interested in representing his client. Therefore, he knew that he had to act aggressively on Olivia's behalf. The competing agent was disheartened to hear that he had lost the deal. He assumed that all parties would follow conventional rules, and he was caught off guard when his competitor made a savvy business move.

In fact, after finding out, he was convinced that Max, the seller's agent, or both of them had acted unethically. Therefore, he pushed to have the details of the transaction subpoenaed. Both Max and the seller were confident that the accusations were baseless. In the end, the charges were dropped. If there were any misstep at all, it was that the competing agent had waited too long for Max's mind to figure out a way to win yet another listing along Malibu's beachfront.

In this scenario just described, Max was able to earn the listing for Olivia for three reasons: knowledge, connections, and experience.

## KNOWLEDGE

Knowledge answers the question, "How well does my real estate agent know the area where I plan to buy?" Once Olivia phoned Max, he immediately found a property that met her needs. Because he was an expert in Malibu beachfront property, he was able to find the home she wanted. In fact, Olivia trusted him so much that she authorized him to make an offer on the house without even seeing it herself.

Trust is critical when you are buying high-end property. Real estate agents with years of experience pride themselves on their client's confidence in them.

As I indicated in the beginning of this chapter, with almost 20 beach communities along Malibu's coastline, your options can become complicated. Therefore, there are many choices and many differences from area to area that only an experienced agent will understand. Furthermore, with an agent who specializes in beachfront property and has years of working knowledge of the area, you have access to listings that aren't widely advertised, if advertised at all. You also have a source of information about the features of each neighborhood: Is it a good place to raise children? Is it prone to mudslides? Or is there a lot of public foot traffic along the beach? Throughout your search, your agent will become not only the one looking for your listings, but a valuable resource for questions that you will have.

## CONNECTIONS

Max was a skilled agent. His competitor had an equally solid reputation in Malibu. In these instances, when two experienced agents are working to win a listing, the competition is fierce. Although both agents were well connected in the area, Max's connections were better. His relationship with the seller's agent was key to winning the deal. Once she shared that the second buyer requested another showing, Max and his assistant went to work to figure out how this could help Olivia buy the home. With this bit of information, Max's assistant realized why the competing agent was on the property that Thursday afternoon.

Once Max's assistant phoned him, he tapped into his years of negotiation experience. He realized the leverage he had and how this was critical to write his final offer. Keep in mind that negotiation involves giving the other party a reason to accept your offer. The question the seller was asking himself was, "What's in it for me?" Therefore, Max had to provide a price that would entice the seller and at the same time save Olivia money. He knew that the offer had to be simple—30-day escrow and all cash—in order for the seller to want to respond by the 5:00 p.m. deadline. An agent with less experience, or with less aggressive negotiation skills, would have waited until Friday, giving the seller two offers to consider. Instead, Max turned the tables on the seller and gave Olivia the advantage.

In addition, connections are important for another reason. As I explained in Chapter 2, in Malibu, not all listings are made public. Sometimes a home may go for sale and is never put on the MLS (Multiple Listing Service). And in beachfront areas, where property is limited, your agent's contacts will get you the property you want. Your agent's knowledge of the beachfront area, combined with her connections, can make the difference between finding a house that you'll love at first sight and one that you'll buy because you thought that there was nothing else available. Sadly, when people rely on mediocre agents, they buy without ever knowing that they could have purchased something better.

## EXPERIENCE

Although this was certainly a real estate coup for Max, it was by no means his first. In the end, his ability to act swiftly and calmly was what made the purchase a success. Certainly, some agents work swiftly, but if decisions are made impulsively, the result can be a lost deal. Furthermore, if your agent only works calmly, you could miss out on a listing that has the possibility to make you a healthy profit. In most cases, the two qualities—swiftness and calmness—only come through years of experience. After all, it takes many, many real estate transactions for an agent to act on changes as they arise.

Max knew that the seller's agent had provided him with important information. Once his assistant let him know about the second showing, he quickly realized that he could turn this otherwise difficult situation into one that gave Olivia the advantage.

## WHEN YOU TRUST YOUR AGENT,
## HE CAN MAKE YOU MILLIONS

As a final note, once Olivia bought the home, Max continued to work hard for her. As you recall, Max suggested that Olivia upgrade the home. What made this difficult was the fact that Olivia lived across the country. Therefore, Olivia would not be present for the majority of the renovation. Fortunately, she knew that Max had reliable connections in the construction industry, so Olivia left the project up to him. Talk about trusting your real estate agent.

Max spent the next couple of months coordinating the renovation. The changes were significant. He added new wood floors, carpet, and a touch screen system that controlled the audio-visual, HVAC, and lighting throughout the home. In addition, he landscaped and painted the property inside and out. The final cost of the project was $250,000. Remember, Olivia purchased the home for $5.2 million. To that, she spent $250,000 on upgrades. Afterwards, she sold it for $9.5 million, which meant that she earned a profit of almost $4 million dollars from an investment she made from across the country. Good agents definitely know how to make their clients money.

I've given you examples of what the best agents do for their clients. If there is one message I would like you to remember it is this: top agents go far beyond your expectations. If you recall, at the beginning of this chapter, Kathleen removed the unsightly fake foliage from the exterior of the home. She only did this because her number one priority was to sell the home. Agents who are less committed or overworked will not take the time to make last minute changes like she did. And in the end, her decision made the difference between a home that sold and one that remained on the market. And in Olivia's case, her trust in Max ultimately earned her a $4 million dollar profit.

In the next chapter, we'll explore what you need to know when you are hiring an agent. I'll give you a list of four questions to ask when you're looking for the best real estate agent to represent you in your beachfront purchase.

# FINDING THE RIGHT
# BUYER'S AGENT
*The Top Four Questions to Ask*

O ver the years, I have seen real estate agents come and go. Indeed, the real estate industry is notorious for its high turnover rate. Therefore, when you're looking for an agent to help you buy your beachfront property, it's important to find one who really knows what he's doing, rather than one whose name you simply got from a notepad with his picture on it. In this section, I'll guide you through the process of selecting the right agent to take care of your beachfront property search.

It continually amazes me how buyers will often spend more time selecting an interior decorator than the agent who will handle one of the biggest investments of their lives. Regardless of whether it's a two-bedroom condominium in the Las Tunas or a $20 million home in Carbon Beach, too many buyers fail to commit the time to find an agent who will represent them.

At this point, you need to know the difference between an agent who has a solid reputation in the community and one who is well known because of his marketing skills. A good self-promoter knows how to create name recognition for himself. He may have slick marketing materials, such as print ads and a Web site, and he may even be well known throughout the city. This doesn't necessarily mean that he's an experienced agent. In addition, you must get along well with your agent. But this is just the beginning. You must keep in mind that just because you have good rapport with an agent this does not mean that he will act aggressively when you need a tough negotiator.

In addition, many buyers continue to work with an agent because they have been doing so for years. Certainly, if your agent has been satisfactory over many years, he is probably good at what he does. But remember to always keep your options open.

### CONNECTING WITH YOUR AGENT IS A GOOD FIRST STEP, BUT IT'S ONLY A FIRST STEP

The real estate profession is filled with agents with top-notch rapport skills but who lack solid business experience. The beachfront is no exception. When a colleague and I were discussing the matter, he expressed it in terms that drove the message home.

"People pick agents like they pick cars," he began. "When you see an ugly car on the road, you think, 'Who would ever pick a car like that?' But then you realize that someone did pick that car and probably likes it; and secondly, someone is looking at your car and thinking the same thing."

I too have seen the same phenomenon in real estate. Agents who have poor negotiation skills and lack professionalism still manage to get clients. I believe this is because people often select agents based only on emotional reasons. An agent who has communication skills is not enough. He must also possess the qualities of experience and knowledge and have a wide network of associates. On the other hand, an agent who has solid business skills is not enough either. Regardless of how well he knows how to crunch numbers and knows the beachfront market, if you have difficulty getting along with him, most likely others will as well. An agent with both rapport skills and experience is your best combination.

## THE TITLE "REAL ESTATE AGENT" DOESN'T MEAN HE IS THE MOST QUALIFIED

I know agents who were shampooing carpets the year before, sank tens of thousands of dollars into promoting themselves, and now have multi-million dollar listings—with virtually no real estate experience. The trust that buyers and sellers of real estate give to people about whom they know almost nothing continues to surprise me. A simple question such as, "How many beachfront properties have you sold within the last 12 months?" would quickly separate experienced agents from last year's waiters and auto mechanics.

Some agents have virtual celebrity status in the circles where they work. For many, this image has been earned through years of hard work. Other times it has more to do with savvy marketing skills. In either case, clients are drawn to them because they have seen their listings in fancy magazines or have heard about them from others. But instead of simply relying on their marketing materials, do a bit more research. This small additional investment of your time will make your home search go faster and save you money.

Let me share about an agent who specializes in high-end real estate. Rachel spends tens of thousands of dollars each year filling the prestigious real estate magazines with her listings. In addition, she markets herself as the "Top Producer" in her exclusive area. She has effectively convinced the public that she is the best agent. For instance, because of her reputation, sellers will ask their agents to co-list with her. They believe that having her name appear below their listing will bring in buyers. Now, with almost no work on her part, Rachel gets a cut of the commission and is able to calculate the home into her "Year-to-Date" sales figure. Unfortunately, this does little to help the buyer or the seller.

Beachfront property is high-stakes business. In the end, it does not matter whose name appears in more ads. Here are four questions you should ask when selecting an agent to represent you in your purchase:

1. What kinds of listings has the agent helped her or his clients purchase?
2. Does the agent specialize in the type of property that you're looking for?
3. How extensive are her or his comparables?
4. Has the agent been involved in any lawsuits?

## 1. WHAT KINDS OF LISTINGS HAS THE AGENT HELPED HER OR HIS BUYERS PURCHASE?

This question has to do with an agent's negotiation skills. Her ability to quickly respond to events as they come up—and in real estate, circumstances can change within minutes—is what will get you the home you want. Throughout the transaction, your agent will be negotiating on your behalf about not only price but also contingencies and the escrow period. Therefore, you want to make sure that regardless of how easy or difficult your home purchase is, your agent will be able to handle situations that arise. Here is where her years of experience become particularly important.

## 2. DOES THE AGENT SPECIALIZE IN THE TYPE OF PROPERTY THAT YOU'RE LOOKING FOR?

If you're interested in buying a parcel of land, you want to work with someone who specializes in buying and selling land. For example, an agent who is an expert at buying land will know about the permit process, the stages of land approval, the various geological tests, the percolation tests for septic systems, and more. And if you're looking to buy in Bel Air, you want an agent who specializes in that area. The same goes for beachfront property.

Imagine that you're considering purchasing a home that lists for $1 million. You decide to work with an agent whom you've known for years. He is highly experienced and has bought and sold many homes for you. Unfortunately, he has limited knowledge of Malibu's beachfront. Despite this, you are confident that because of his professional experience, he can easily handle this purchase.

Based on his non-Malibu comparables, he suggests that you offer $975,000, or $25,000 off the list price. You think that saving $25,000 dollars is a sound idea, and you authorize him to move ahead. Afterwards, another buyer submits an offer as well. The deal now has multiple offers (or multiples), and the competition begins.

Or instead, you decide to work with an agent who specializes in Malibu beachfront property. The agent finds you the same $1 million dollar listing. You see the home and you want to buy it. The agent does his research and tells you that the price is a steal—based on his comparables, ones that only he has, the last home in the area sold for $1.2 million. The seller's $1 million listing price indicates that the owner wants to either sell quickly, or she simply doesn't have access to comparables that your agent does. He suggests that you offer full price. At first, you are hesitant, but then your agent shows you the comparables. In addition, he warns that anything below $1 million may take the sale into multiples. You agree to offer at full price. The seller accepts your offer; you save $200,000 and avoid multiples.

An experienced agent will be able to distinguish between a listing price and the quantifiable value of the home. In the example described above, the $1 million house was undervalued. The buyer's agent who specialized in Malibu's beachfront had access to comparables that indicated that the house could have sold for $1.2 million. Another way to state this is that the agent knew the difference between the subjective and objective prices and negotiated accordingly.

A subjective price is the amount for which the owner has agreed to sell the property. For example, the agent will tell her client, "Your home would sell for $5 million based on comparables." The seller may agree, but like many investors, the owner wants to see if he can sell it for more. Therefore, the price that he eventually lists may not be an accurate amount that the home is really worth. On the other hand, the quantifiable value, or objective price of the home, considers comparables, location, square footage, layout, and age in deciding how much the home is worth.

In other instances, buyers will often meet with a seller's agent and realize that the other agent knows more about the area than the person they are working with.

For instance, a colleague shares a story about a businessman who was leasing in Carbon Beach. Larry had lived there for a couple of years and realized that Malibu's beachfront was where he wanted to permanently settle. After his lease was up, Larry was considering buying a home in nearby La Costa or in Carbon itself. His agent arranged for a showing of a beachfront home. When they arrived, they met with Robert, the seller's agent. Robert showed them the listing, shared information about the sales of nearby homes, and was able to answer questions regarding the home's foundation, septic system, and zoning. Throughout the meeting, Larry's agent stood silently and listened because he had little to contribute to the conversation.

That afternoon, Larry showed up at Robert's office. He was relieved to finally find him. After their meeting at the La Costa house, Larry had driven up and down PCH looking for Robert. Earlier that afternoon, he walked into one of Malibu's biggest real estate companies hoping to find him there. Although Robert didn't work for that company, most people in the real estate community knew who he was. Therefore, an agent was able to direct him to the right office.

When they met, Larry told him how impressed he was with his knowledge of the area. During the showing of the La Costa property, it was clear which real estate agent knew more about beachfront real estate. Therefore, he was convinced that Robert could serve him better than his current real estate agent. Larry switched real estate agents, and Robert found him exactly what he wanted. Eventually, he moved to La Costa. Larry has been a satisfied client ever since.

### 3. HOW EXTENSIVE ARE HER OR HIS COMPARABLES?

Along Malibu's beachfront, comparables are an experienced agent's best-kept secret. If your agent does not specialize in Malibu's coastal property, you may be missing out on critical information. After all, you want to know that the list price accurately represents the market value of the house, and comparables are the best way to determine this.

Through comparables, your agent will know whether the price of a home truly reflects the amount for which similar homes in the area have sold. An agent who has extensive comparables can tell you whether the sellers are offering the listing at a reasonable price. For example, many sellers will test the market by offering a home way above the comparables. Your agent will only know this if she has access to all comparables, including ones that are not made available to the public. This is critical information when you are drafting an offer.

## 4. HAS THE AGENT BEEN INVOLVED IN ANY LAWSUITS?

Make sure that your agent and his broker have not been involved in legal battles for matters that could put your purchase at risk. Ask the agent. If you aren't satisfied with his answer, ask others in the real estate profession. In Malibu, information about lawsuits spreads quickly.

For review, here are the most important questions to ask your agent:

1. What kinds of listings has the agent helped her or his buyers purchase?
2. Does the agent specialize in the type of property you're looking for?
3. How extensive are her or his comparables?
4. Has the agent been involved in any lawsuits?

Allow me to add one additional point that I addressed in a previous chapter. When you are looking for an agent, ask her about multiple offers. What kind of track record does she have when competing for a listing with other agents? Winning a listing in a highly competitive multiple-offer setting is a good sign of an agent's ability to negotiate effectively on your behalf.

A real estate agent with a solid reputation is creative and thinks quickly when things become complicated. Make sure that your agent knows how to win a hot listing.

The time that you invest in finding the best agent will reward you over and over again. Your agent will find the properties that best fit your needs; she will effectively negotiate on your behalf; and she will steer you away from potential legal pitfalls. Now that you know how to find a good agent to represent you in your purchase, in the next chapter I'll guide you through the escrow process.

# ESCROW

*The Home Stretch*

I n the purchase and sale of real estate the term escrow refers to the money and documents deposited to a third party (an escrow company). Upon closing, when the buyer and seller have fulfilled their responsibilities, the escrow officer will disperse the money and paperwork to the bank, mortgage company, and all other involved parties.

Therefore, escrow companies have a significant responsibility in your real estate transaction. A company that really knows the business will make your purchase or sale go smoothly and protect you from legal problems. On the other hand, a company that cuts corners and works negligently can get you into trouble. The following example illustrates how a bad escrow company can create problems for you.

A colleague tells me the story of a client who was looking to buy in the Colony. Laura was a former television star, a mother of two children, and came from one of the wealthiest and well-known families in the country. Taylor, her agent, had found her a home that met her needs, and when her client saw it, she was pleased. Laura and the seller agreed on a purchase price. On March 5th, the home went into escrow, and Laura deposited 3 percent of the home's sale price.

Unfortunately, Laura was also in the middle of a messy divorce. Her attorney advised her that if she purchased a home before the divorce was finalized, her husband could lay claim to the property. Therefore, her mother, who would ultimately take a small piece of the family fortune to pay for the home, asked her daughter to back out of the deal. Laura listened to the advice of her lawyer and her mother and withdrew her offer.

## THE 17-DAY CONTINGENCY PERIOD

The first 17 days of an escrow are usually called a contingency period. Between day one through 17, the buyer typically has the home inspected. At this stage, backing out of the purchase is a simple matter. On the 18th day, whether the buyer responds or not, it is implied that she has accepted the terms of the sale. If a buyer wants to end the deal after this point, the 3 percent deposit will most likely go to the seller.

Before the 17 days are up, however, the buyer can back out for any number of reasons. She can say that she didn't agree with the physical inspection, or after reviewing the inspection she thought that the home needed too many repairs.

On March 22nd, the 17th day after the start of escrow, Laura told her agent that she no longer wanted the home. Immediately after hearing the news, Taylor stood in the real estate office's workroom and fed two sheets of paper into the fax machine: a cover letter and a document that specified that Laura was no longer interested in buying the home. The paperwork was routine—she had delivered countless letters like these over the course of her career. Once the fax was sent, a confirmation slip followed, but Taylor didn't bother to take it with her.

The next day, the seller's agent phoned Taylor and claimed that the buyer responded on the 23rd, not the 22nd. The difference between one day meant that the escrow company believed that Laura agreed to move ahead with the sale. Taylor explained that Laura didn't want the home anymore.

The seller honored her request to end the deal but insisted that the buyer should not get her 3 percent deposit back. Taylor knew that the seller's claims were groundless. After all, she had sent a fax on March 22nd—day 17. Unfortunately, she did not have a confirmation slip to verify that the fax was indeed sent on the 17th day. What she did have was a cover letter with a written date that the fax was sent. But this wasn't enough—anyone can create a cover letter after the fact.

What Taylor needed was the confirmation slip. But when she looked around the workroom, the key piece of paper was nowhere. She and her assistant then looked in the recycle bin, but it had already been emptied. The two knew that this slip of paper would quickly end the seller's silly claims, but they didn't know where it was. Fortunately, it was still early in the week, and the trash had not yet been collected. Taylor and her assistant realized that they had only one choice—excavate the office's garbage.

Was the person who saw the slip sitting by the fax machine a good steward of the Earth and toss it into the workroom's recycle bin? Or did he throw it in the trashcan stuffed with stale coffee, banana peels, and balls of Kleenex? This was the one day Taylor hoped that whoever threw the paper away let his green instincts prevail. After all, looking through sheets of commingled paper is a far more pleasant task than rummaging through the office's undesirables.

She and her assistant set out for the trash bins in the back of the office. Once there, they put on latex gloves and foraged through the recycled trash. Several times Taylor would declare, "I found it!" only to discover that it was someone else's slip. They looked through the entire bin but had not uncovered the piece of paper that would save the day.

Still uncertain about whether the paper was tossed into the regular or recycled trash, they decided to look through the office's garbage. They ripped apart the translucent plastic skin that neatly enclosed left-over lunches and wads of gum. Bag after bag was torn, and after all of them had been opened, there was still no confirmation paper.

Had that simple slip of paper been in her hands, Taylor knew that the seller's claim would be groundless. At this time, the lawyers from the seller's side were establishing timelines and therefore requested that Taylor and Laura hand over all documents related to the transaction. To protect their interests, Laura's family filed a counter suit. If the charges were determined to be frivolous, the counter suit would cover attorney fees and interest on the 3 percent deposit that was now frozen. Laura's attorney informed Taylor that the simplest way to have the charges dropped was to prove that the document was sent on time.

Taylor repeatedly phoned the escrow office and asked to speak with the officer who managed the seller's sale. During each phone call, the secretary would tell her that the officer was either not in or was too busy to speak with her. Taylor was resolute and continued to pursue the matter. After persistent phone calls to the escrow office, the secretary told Taylor the exact date and time that the escrow officer would be in her office.

The savvy real estate agent had a plan. On the day of the phone appointment, as she was speaking with the escrow officer, her assistant,

Mike, would drive to the escrow office. When Mike showed up, the secretary could not claim that the officer was not in, because he would tell her that Taylor had just spoken with her. He would then meet with her and finally see the fax for himself.

On the day of the appointment, Taylor phoned the officer. Meanwhile, Mike drove to the escrow office. While on the phone, Taylor asked about the fax, and Jennifer, the officer, stuck with the story and said that she received it on the 18th day. As they were on the phone, Mike arrived at the office. He walked into the reception area and asked the secretary if he could meet with Jennifer.

"I'm sorry, she's out right now," the secretary told him.

"Actually, I know she's here because she just spoke with my boss," he said.

The secretary phoned Jennifer and told her that Mike was waiting outside of her office. With no excuse and caught completely by surprise, she let him in.

"Hello Jennifer. I'm Mike; we've spoken on the phone before. I wanted to know if I could have copies of the fax that you received from us," he said.

Jennifer shifted in her seat and erratically fumbled through paperwork on her desk.

"Um, well, I wasn't expecting to see you right now," she said, looking down at her desk.

Mike knew that he had caught her in a panicked state. She had no time to formulate a plan, make up a convincing excuse, or tell a smooth lie. And regardless of how slick she could have been, he was determined to get her to tell the truth.

"Look, all I want is to get copies of the documents that you said you had."

"I don't think I have them right now," she said.

"What do you mean? Where else could they be? Just let me see the fax."

Jennifer was too flustered to think of an excuse, and after fumbling through some papers, she finally confessed that she had the fax with her. She asked him to wait in the lobby while she photocopied it. She then gave him a copy of the document. What she handed Mike was a copy of the original fax that Taylor had sent, but the document had clearly been altered. Marks on the copy showed that she had cut and pasted a new date on the original fax.

Mike immediately saw that the fax had been changed. With this, the missing fax confirmation sheet was unnecessary, and the seller's accusations were now baseless. Within days after handing the fax to Laura's attorney, the charges were dropped.

Despite trying its best, the escrow company couldn't hide the truth. After legal fees and interest on Laura's 3 percent deposit, it ended up costing the seller and the escrow company a good deal of money.

## EXPENSIVE OR CHEAP, PRICE DOESN'T MATTER

While not all escrow companies will hide information like Jennifer's company did, you want to be careful whom you work with. For instance, some escrow companies offer rock-bottom rates, but they may be slow to return phone calls—or worse, they may have sloppy accounting practices. Others are expensive because they have the reputation of being exclusive, but they really don't provide service that is any different from their competitors.

What you need in an escrow company is one that will return your phone calls quickly, understand the law, and know the stages of an escrow period. The last point may seem silly to even state, but many escrow companies don't work efficiently.

In your home purchase, you may not know the best escrow company to work with. Unless you're buying and selling several times a year, your experience with escrow companies will only come a few times over your entire life. If you aren't interested in investing hours in creating a list of questions to ask your escrow company, or interviewing the office, you will probably just go with whom your agent recommends or with a company that a friend refers you to. These are both fast ways to find an escrow officer.

Here is where your agent will play a key role. If you've invested the time into finding a good agent by following the guidelines in this book, your agent will be a good source to suggest an escrow company. As a quick review to what makes a good agent, you want to make sure that he or she has a reputation within the community, a long list of satisfied customers, limits the number of clients he or she will take, and—this is a key point—neither the real estate agent or broker has a reputation for being involved in court cases.

In addition, make sure that the agent provides you with his recommendation but gives you names of other companies with which to work as well. You want to make sure that the agent is serving your best interest, not his.

Your escrow company will protect you from liability, will make your sale or purchase go smoothly, and will answer your questions promptly. On the other hand, a sloppy, or worse, an unscrupulous escrow officer will create stress in your life and possibly get you into legal trouble.

Now that we've covered the purchase and sale of beachfront property, I'll describe how your coastal investment can generate a substantial income, while you still own it. In the next chapter, I'll explain all you need to know to have a successful lease.

# GETTING THE MOST FROM YOUR BEACHFRONT LEASE

When you buy along Malibu's beachfront, you are investing in some of the world's most exclusive property. Therefore, your investment can give you incredible returns when you sell. Even without selling, however, your beachfront property can generate hefty profits. For instance, during the summer months, a 2,000 square foot home in the Malibu Colony can lease for $50,000 per month.

Here is an example of a lease that a colleague shared with me. An R&B star from Oakland, California was recording an album in Los Angeles. During his month-long stay, he wanted a large home for his crew and himself. A real estate agent was showing the artist's business manager different properties in Malibu. One in particular, a 11,000 square foot home in Carbon Beach, drew the manager's attention. It was available for $160,000 a month. Not only was its beachfront location the perfect place for the celebrity and his entourage, but it was also within walking distance to several fast-food restaurants. The business manager knew that the easy access to fried chicken and hamburgers would appeal to his client.

Unfortunately, the owner was not interested in leasing the home for only a month. The singer ended up finding a home that rented for

$120,000 per month in another Malibu beach. Thanks to the secluded location of the home and 24-hour bodyguards, he and his crew had a safe stay.

Of course, most properties along Malibu's beachfront don't lease for $160,000 per month. But regardless of how big or small your monthly fees are, owning along Malibu's beachfront can generate a large profit.

The lure of leasing is clear. While you're away on a European vacation, your tenants are paying for your trip through their monthly rent. Or, if your beachfront house is your second, third, or fourth home, you earn money from a residence that would otherwise sit empty. But because the profits can be so high, many homeowners make the mistake of thinking that a lease is an easy way to earn money.

The fact is that leases are not easy. If you plan to earn $60,000 per month or more for your home, it is going to take effort on your part. In this chapter, I'll explain benefits of leasing that you may have not considered. In addition, I'll describe the pitfalls you may encounter and ways to make the process as profitable and headache-free for you as possible.

## LEASING IS HELPFUL WHEN YOU PLAN TO SELL

The obvious reason for leasing is the opportunity to earn a substantial profit. During the summer months, a home that would normally lease for $5,000 could rent for $12–15 thousand per month, while homes in The Colony could fetch as much as $75,000 per month during the summer peak.

Aside from the significant income you can earn through a lease, there are other reasons why they are a good idea. A lease can lead to a sale. If you eventually want to sell and the tenant wants to purchase a home, you have an instant buyer. This is where a good relationship between you and your tenant is key—the tenant chooses to lease the home because he likes it, and you lease to him because he pays on time and takes good care of your property.

For instance, I had a client who leased the same property every summer. Over the years, he and the tenant got to know each other well. Both treated the home with great care. When the owner decided to sell, he didn't have to list it because he already had a buyer waiting. Meanwhile, the buyer knew exactly what he was purchasing because he had lived there for several summers. The sale ended quickly, and both parties were satisfied.

## LEASING PITFALLS

As I described earlier, the most common mistake people make when leasing their home is thinking that the process will be simple. As a result, the homeowner will leave the job to a mediocre agent. The reality is that when you lease your home, the paperwork and preparation involved can rival that of a home's sale. Therefore, the agent you choose to work with will make the difference between an experience that you would like to have every year and one that brings constant complaints from an unsatisfied tenant. A good agent will not only make the process as smooth as possible but will protect you from potential problems.

First of all, when you're preparing to lease your home, you want to make sure that everything in it is working properly. This may seem obvious, but for owners who don't call their beachfront home their primary residence, they may not know what is or isn't working.

For this reason, when my clients are preparing to lease their homes, I provide them with a checklist. (You'll find a version of this at the end of this chapter.) The items on the list come from years of experience. Much of what I learned came through clients getting upset over matters as simple as missing hangers in the closet. To avoid angry phone calls from your tenants, check off every item on the list.

## FROM SATELLITE TV PROBLEMS TO HVAC REPAIRS, YOUR AGENT WILL OFTEN SAVE THE DAY

An agent who has been handing leases for years knows what to expect. And if you've never leased your home before, there are many factors that you might not have considered. Instead of waiting for things to go wrong, an experienced agent will anticipate potential problems and resolve them beforehand.

For instance, does your home have an iron? Are there two sets of clean sheets? Is your garage door working? You would be surprised how one small detail can make a tenant's experience unpleasant. And if you're on a cruise in the Caribbean or live in another state when your tenant calls with a concern, you had better have someone in Malibu committed to resolving the problem. Many times that person is your real estate agent. Experienced agents have countless stories of last-minute trips to Target to buy toilet paper or drives across town scrambling to find a universal remote control because the one at home was not working.

For example, a colleague of mine received a phone call from a tenant. She told the agent that the satellite TV system was broken. When the agent phoned the company, the representative told him that a technician could be there within four days. Now imagine you were paying $60,000 to stay in a home for the month of June. If you divide 30-days by $60,000, you are paying $2,000 per day to lease. At this rate, you should expect to have the television working every day you are there.

The agent could not wait four days for the satellite company to fix the problem. Therefore, he decided to get the system running himself. Up to this point, his experience setting up satellite systems went no further than pushing the red "power" button at the top of the remote control. He realized, however, that the tenant's needs came first. He spent half the day with technical support on the other end of the phone to fix the satellite system.

On another occasion, the same tenant phoned the real estate agent, furious that the garage door wouldn't open. His frustration was understandable considering that along PCH parking can be difficult—especially during the summer months. The agent arrived at the home and pressed the button on the remote transmitter. The door wouldn't budge. He phoned a garage door company. The technician came to the home and examined the door. He determined that the opener's motor was too small. The agent now had the responsibility of replacing the entire garage door mechanism.

When you're looking for a real estate agent to handle your lease, many agents will say that they can handle it, but when there is a problem, they may not know what to do. So make sure you ask what kind of experience the agent has with beachfront leases.

## HOW TO SHOW A HOME TO PROSPECTIVE TENANTS

Your agent will request that you make your home look as inviting as possible for potential tenants. This means that you present your home in a way that will attract those who are willing to pay top dollar for a beachfront lease. For summer leases, tenants may look as early as January. Most of the time, however, they begin looking between March and April. Here again is where experience counts. An agent who has worked with leases for many years will have a large pool of quality tenants. This will not only make finding a tenant faster, but will give you peace of mind as you pass the keys and the security code to her.

A colleague shares a story about a couple from England who were looking to rent in The Colony. The two heard about the real estate agent from a friend. During their meeting, Mark, the agent, shared information about some of the homes available for lease in this exclusive area. He retells the conversation.

"Well, as you know, the Colony is home to many Hollywood celebrities," Mark recalls saying.

"I'm really not interested in hearing about these people. It's such an American thing, you know, this obsession with celebrity," the English man said.

Mark then asked about the couple's finances, in other words, what they could pay.

"Well, I'm a Lord," the man said.

Mark laughed, thinking that the man was saying the equivalent of the American expression, "I'm the Man." That is to say, "I could pay whatever you need." His laughter was followed by an awkward silence.

Mark then took the couple to visit homes. He drove to the security gate, cleared himself with the guard, and entered The Colony. As they were in the car, he pointed out a couple of the homes that were available for lease.

"Homes in The Colony can easily rent for $50,000 per month," he told them.

"You can't be serious," said the Lord. "These homes? Back home we'd call them shanties."

Suddenly, the Lord spotted a famous American rock star get out of his car.

"I know him!" the Lord said, as he pointed to the celebrity. Reacting like a Malibu High teenager spotting Brittany Spears at Zuma Beach, he asked, "Can you slow down the car?"

Mark carried out his request so the Lord could take a long look at the musician. The real estate agent was amused by the Lord's reaction. Obviously, Americans aren't the only ones who get excited when they see a famous person. The couple ended up leasing a home in The Colony. Perhaps, for the Lord, having his favorite rock star live nearby made the homes seem less like housing projects.

## HOW MUCH IS YOUR HOME WORTH?

Determining the price of your lease is similar to figuring out how much to sell your home for. Comparables will give you a good idea of what you can charge. In addition, negotiation is typically involved. The lease market changes from year to year and season to season. Thus, prices fluctuate.

The level of service that your agent provides is key to making the lease a success. An agent who knows the beachfront real estate market knows exactly what steps are involved in the lease process. Think of a good agent like you would a reliable CPA. While the mediocre accountant will simply take all of your paperwork and process your taxes, an experienced CPA will look over your financial statements and figure out the best way to minimize your tax consequences.

Similarly, a good agent plays the role of service provider as well as consultant. She will answer all of your questions, create timelines and schedules, and protect you from liability. For instance, at the end of a lease, imagine that you discover that your favorite vase is chipped. You bring this up to the tenant, and he says that it was broken before he moved in. Fortunately, your agent took pictures of your home prior to the tenant's arrival. The vase appears in the photos, unbroken. The tenant will now be responsible to pay for it.

In one instance, an agent shared with me about the time his client returned to her home to find that the dining room rug had shrunk. It was obvious to the owner because she could see more of the travertine floor underneath than she could before.

Tim, the agent, phoned the tenant about the matter, and she denied knowing anything about what had happened. At this point, Tim pulled out the digital recording he made of the home before the owners left on their three-month cruise. In the digital footage, the size of the rug was clear. When compared to the current area, the rug was now smaller.

Again, Tim contacted the former tenant. "I've looked over a recording of the house I made, and it's pretty obvious that the rug is smaller. Are you sure that nothing happened?"

"I really don't remember. I did so much work at the end to make sure it looked good. Maybe I sent it out to get cleaned," the tenant said.

"You mean you don't remember if you had the rug removed?" Tim asked.

"Oh yes, I think I did. Maybe I spilled something," she said.

"Like what?" Tim asked.

"I don't know, maybe one of my dogs spilled something," the tenant said.

"Dogs? It was clearly stated in the paperwork that pets weren't allowed," the agent said.

Afterwards, the tenant confessed that one of her dogs had relieved himself on the rug and that she tried to get rid of the spot by having it professionally cleaned. The tenant paid for a replacement rug. If Tim had not walked through the home with a camera in hand, the rug would have most likely not been replaced.

## THE RIGHT MINDSET IS KEY TO A SUCCESSFUL LEASE

Leases can turn into a huge headache for the landlord, the tenant, and the agents involved. After all, this is not just a business decision—emotions come into play as well. Homeowners are uncomfortable thinking about someone living in their home while they are away; the tenant's expectations are high because they are paying top dollar to rent a home that is not theirs.

In addition, many homeowners become complacent about their role as landlord—either they are uncomfortable with being one or they are just not prepared for the responsibility. Whichever the case, the result can make the process unpleasant for everyone. A landlord may become frustrated with a tenant's complaint that a light bulb is out. "What's the tenant's problem? It's no big deal, and he should be happy with the home as it is," landlords often tell me.

What I have to remind them is that the tenant is paying a huge premium to rent along the beachfront. Therefore, the complaint about the light bulb or leaky faucet is understandable. The bottom line is that once you decide to lease your home, you become a landlord. And the potential for substantial profits means that you must be willing to take care of your tenants.

Before a tenant moves in, landlords will often be asked to resolve matters that require a lot of work. Case in point: A friend of mine represented a landlord who owned a home in Encinal Bluffs. The tenant agreed to pay $53,000 per month for June, July, and August. The tenant was sensitive to animal hair, and the landlord had several dogs. Two weeks before the owner left her home, she used air purifiers to rid the home of animal dander and the pet smell. She also hired cleaners to remove the dog hair from the house. In other instances, a tenant may want to bring in his own bed and hang his artwork on the walls. The landlord may balk at this suggestion, not realizing that a lease requires sacrifices from both the owner and the tenant.

On the other hand, leases are more flexible than purchase agreements. In a home sale, for instance, everything is clearly stated. There is no room to maneuver. If an escrow closes on the third of the month, all parties must have their paperwork ready on that day. Leases, on the other hand, can last for a couple of days or a few months. They can have conditions about furniture, pets, or smoking. But regardless of how detailed the agreement is, you can't possibly cover everything in a contract. If the landlord states that he will not allow smoking in the house, it will be almost impossible to monitor whether the tenant followed through with his request.

## THE SECRET TO A SUCCESSFUL LEASE

Your beachfront property draws people willing to pay top dollar for a spectacular view of the ocean or quick access to the coast. Therefore, a beachfront lease is a way to earn a significant income while still owning your home.

Done correctly, you will have an experience that is worth your investment of time and money. But if you approach a lease with little planning, you can have days, weeks, or months of complaints coming from an unhappy tenant. Or even worse, you may have a lawsuit on your hands.

The key to making your rental a success is to choose an agent who has years of experience with beachfront leases. He will advise you on how to prepare your home, anticipate problems before they arise, and give you expert advice during difficult situations.

Of course, there are no guarantees that you will earn $60,000 per month, have a happy tenant, and move back in after the end of the lease agreement without any problems. But working with a good agent will contribute to having a positive lease experience. When you take the time to find an experienced beachfront agent to handle your lease, you are taking one of the most important steps towards earning the most from your investment.

*Buy The Beach Inc.*

## For The Bedroom

- ❑ Bed frame and mattress
- ❑ Mattress Pad
- ❑ 2 sets of bedsheets
- ❑ Sleeping pillows
- ❑ Blanket or comforter
- ❑ Bedspreads or quilts
- ❑ Bedside table
- ❑ Dresser, chest of drawers
- ❑ Full-length mirror
- ❑ Bookcase
- ❑ Reading light
- ❑ Alarm clock
- ❑ Throw rug
- ❑ Wastebasket
- ❑ Electric Fan
- ❑ Small electric heater
- ❑ Shoe rack
- ❑ Clothes hooks
- ❑ Clothes hangers
- ❑ Plastic under-bed storage containers

## For The Bath

- ❑ 2 sets of towels (bath, hand towels and washclothes)
- ❑ Bath rug
- ❑ Bath mat
- ❑ Shower curtain, rings, liner
- ❑ Bathroom mirror
- ❑ Soap dish
- ❑ Toothbrush holder

## For The Kitchen, Dining Room

- ❑ Dining table and chairs
- ❑ Tablecloths and placemats
- ❑ 5-piece place settings for four
- ❑ Flatware for six
- ❑ Glasses, tumblers, mugs
- ❑ Wine glasses
- ❑ Water pitcher/filter
- ❑ Sugar and cream set
- ❑ Butter dish
- ❑ Serving bowls, serving platter
- ❑ Plastic food-storage containers
- ❑ Salt and pepper set
- ❑ 2 sets of cloth napkins for four
- ❑ Kitchen towels
- ❑ Dish rack
- ❑ Kitchen sponges, dish cleaners
- ❑ Paper napkin dispenser
- ❑ Cookware (essential pots, frying pans)
- ❑ Cooking, serving utensils
- ❑ Kitchen knife set
- ❑ Teapot, coffee maker
- ❑ Toaster
- ❑ Blender, hand mixer
- ❑ Microwave oven
- ❑ Covered microwave-able and over-safe cookware and serving dishes
- ❑ Trivets
- ❑ Hot pads, ovenmit
- ❑ Trash can

## For General Hone Decor, Comfort and Convenience

- ❑ Couch
- ❑ Easy chair
- ❑ Desk or computer table
- ❑ Desk chair
- ❑ Bookcases
- ❑ Floor lamps
- ❑ Desk light
- ❑ Wall art
- ❑ Magazine rack
- ❑ Telephones
- ❑ Phone numbers for tenant
- ❑ Voice mail access ready
- ❑ DSL, cable installed
- ❑ Television
- ❑ CD/DVD player
- ❑ CD/DVD rack or organizer
- ❑ Throw blanket, afghan

## Other Essentials

- ❑ Garage door openers
- ❑ Security codes
- ❑ HVAC in working order
- ❑ Sewing kit
- ❑ Flashlight
- ❑ Extra batteries
- ❑ Storage boxes
- ❑ Broom
- ❑ Vacuum cleaner
- ❑ Plastic bucket
- ❑ Mop
- ❑ Iron
- ❑ Ironing board

# MALIBU'S BEACHFRONT
*27 Miles of World-Famous Real Estate*

From mudslides, storms, and floods to the occasional closure of Pacific Coast Highway, Malibu's residents tolerate more than their share of unfavorable conditions. In fact, Malibu's beachfront has a reputation the world over for not only its beauty but also its famous and resilient residents who call this place home. What surprises both residents and non-residents alike is that along this 27-mile stretch of PCH, there are almost 20 communities. In this chapter, I'll describe each area's key features.

Before I describe what each section is known for, there are three terms that you need to know: wet beach, dry beach, and partially dry beach. If these terms are new to you, they may sound odd. After all, isn't a beach always wet? But as you'll read, the difference between wet, dry, and partially dry is significant in terms of the value of a beachfront home.

In addition, an understanding of tides is essential when buying or selling beachfront property. When most people use the word tide, they are referring to the rise and fall of the sea level with respect to the land. There are two types of tides—high and low—and they usually occur twice a day. High tide is the maximum water level, and low tide is the minimum water level. Therefore, the word tide refers to the vertical change in the sea surface's height during high and low tides.

The tides you see when you are at the beach mainly occur for two reasons. First, the gravitational pull of heavenly bodies, such as the moon and sun, make the tides change. The second cause of tides is not related to astronomical factors. The shape of the coastline, the depth of the water, the topography of the ocean floor, and the weather all work together to affect the tide.

## WHAT ARE THE DIFFERENCES BETWEEN WET, PARTIALLY DRY, AND DRY BEACHES?

Some of Malibu's beach homes will not have dry sand to walk on unless the tides are extremely low; these beaches I'll refer to as wet beaches.

Homes on partially dry beaches will be dry until the high tides come. These high-low tides will occur usually, but not always, twice a day.

The homes located on dry beaches are typically more expensive because they have more useable land and beachfront.

## FROM EAST TO WEST

Malibu's beachfront runs along Pacific Coast Highway (PCH). This main highway runs from east to west. This may seem strange, because most think that in Malibu, PCH runs south to north. When you look on a map, however, you'll see that Malibu's beachfront runs east to west. This is a big bonus for its beachfront residents. In fact, in commercial property, the most desirable place an employee would want her office is in the southwest corner of the building. Similarly, homes along Malibu's coast can face the ocean and have sunlight all day without being directly hit by the sun's rays in the morning or afternoon.

The major communities along Malibu's beachfront are as follows:

1. Las Tunas
2. Big Rock
3. Las Flores
4. La Costa
5. Carbon Beach
6. Malibu Colony
7. Malibu Road
8. Latigo Shore Drive
9. Malibu Cove Colony
10. Escondido Beach
11. Paradise Cove
12. Pointe Dume Bluffs
13. Broad Beach
14. El Matador Beach
15. Encinal Bluffs
16. County Line

## 1. LAS TUNAS

Las Tunas, or "The Prickly Flower," is known as one of the most affordable beaches in Malibu. There are many condominiums and apartments in this area. The beach is wet and rocky, and there is not much sand. It is on PCH, and the area has been known to have an occasional mudslide.

## 2. BIG ROCK

For the most part, Big Rock is a wet beach, although some small sections are partially dry. It is close to the sea; therefore, waves and water come under the homes. The ground is a combination of both sand and rocks. There are smaller beach homes here as well as condominiums and apartments. Because the mountain is steep along PCH, some of the homes are vulnerable to mudslides.

## 3. LAS FLORES

Las Flores Beach, Spanish for "The Flowers," has a beautiful ocean-front and is gaining the interest of buyers who want to live on the beach in a newer home. This stretch of beach boasts beautiful rock formations in the water. Seals visit these rocks to sun and have their pups. The houses in Las Flores are still a bargain compared to beaches closer to mid-Malibu. Although there are many small, older homes on this beach, they are typically purchased and then upgraded, which is the trend throughout Malibu's beachfront.

In addition to the detached homes, Las Flores has condominiums and apartments, which make great second homes and getaways. The neighbors are known to be friendly, and dogs run freely, as there is no open access to the highway. For this reason, Las Flores is also known by locals as "Dog Beach." I believe that there is potential to make significant returns on your investment when you buy a home here because the property is undervalued.

## 4. LA COSTA (SPANISH FOR "THE COAST")

Who says that the "Trickle Down Effect" is make believe? Ask any La Costa homeowner, and she will tell you that in terms of property value, Carbon Beach has been a good neighbor. Because Carbon Beach has only 71 homes, many people who want to live in this part of Malibu buy in neighboring La Costa instead. (And in recent years, Carbon's ambitious homeowners have been buying adjacent plots of land to expand their homes, which makes it even harder to buy there.) Indeed, the exclusivity of Carbon Beach has trickled east to its less famous neighbor and has brought with it a steady increase in property value.

La Costa is a dry beach. Homes here are mostly single-family, but there are also condominiums at the western end near Duke's Malibu Restaurant. In addition, La Costa is known for its deep sandy cove.

## 5. CARBON BEACH

Carbon Beach is known as "Billionaire's Beach" because of its ten-figure income residents. This area has been home—past and present—to people such as Larry Ellison, CEO of Oracle; Peter Morton, owner of Hard Rock Hotel and Casino; DreamWorks partner Jeffrey Katzenberg; and many other rich and famous people. Its high-profile owners combined with an amazing beach have resulted in shockingly high property values. For example, the home of David Geffen, Dream-Works founding partner, is rumored to be worth about $70 million. In fact, Carbon has the reputation of being the most expensive beachfront area in the country.

The beach has a crescent-like shape. It's a dry beach, but the shore runs deepest in the middle of the crescent. In the center of Carbon, its residents have plenty of coastline to walk on even during the highest tide.

The land parcels are 40 to more than 100 feet wide, but owners have purchased neighboring lots and have created mega-parcels. Some lots are now 150 feet or even 285 feet. This has reduced the number of homes available on Carbon.

For many homeowners along this beach, these are second, third, or more homes. Residents often lease their houses, and their rents can be as high as $175,000 per month during the peak summer season. Carbon Beach also has condominiums and apartments along its western end. Like La Costa, it is located on PCH, which means that the garages of these homes face the busy highway. Parking along the street is limited.

## 6. MALIBU COLONY

Also known as The Colony, Malibu Colony was developed during the 1920's and was originally called The Malibu Movie Colony. Many Hollywood celebrities have called this place home. Like Carbon, these can be second, third, or more properties for their owners. The homes have a unique numbering system including a postal address as well as a number that is exclusive to The Colony. For instance, a home's postal address could be a standard five-digit number, such as 22546; within The Colony, it will be referred to as a smaller number, such as Number 54.

The beach is mostly dry, but there are partially dry areas as well. There are 74 beach homes in this gated community. The lots in The Colony tend to be smaller than in areas like Carbon Beach, La Costa, or Broad Beach.

There are two significant advantages to living in Malibu Colony. First, you are behind a gated community that is guarded by 24-hour security personnel. Second, unlike La Costa, Carbon Beach, and Las Flores, it is located away from PCH, which means that it is not on the busy highway. Therefore, it has a neighborhood atmosphere. (For example, you wouldn't want your children riding their bikes or playing basketball on PCH—this is possible in The Colony.) There is a sea wall between the homes and shore, so you have to descend stairs to reach the beach.

### 7. MALIBU ROAD

Malibu Road is also known as The Old Road because years ago, it was the main road through Malibu. After PCH was built, it was renamed Malibu Road. One of its key features is that it offers a place for its residents to walk and ride their bikes away from the main highway. A particular section is known by the elaborate name "Malibu Colony Outside the Gates." Homes in this section are patrolled by security from The Colony. Years ago, a back gate was installed to secure Malibu Colony Road. It closed off The Colony Road, and Larry Hagman's former home remained inside The Colony. Meanwhile, the former residence of Burgess Meredith became the first property in the "Malibu Colony Outside the Gates" stretch of homes. This section of Malibu Road rivals Carbon in its sizes of lots and homes—some have pools and tennis courts.

The Old Road is about 2.5 miles long. The homes vary greatly: a $10 million home can have a four-plex or a small cottage as its neighbor. (You'll find this to be true on Carbon Beach as well.) Malibu Road has some of Malibu's most expensive condominiums, but you can also find surprisingly affordable apartments.

Malibu Road has many personalities. There are estate-like properties, rocky beachfront areas, sandy strips of scenic land, and actively
moving slide areas. Its central setting in Malibu adds to its appeal because residents can walk to shops and restaurants. The prime location of
homes along Malibu Road makes this a sought-after place to live.

## 8. LATIGO SHORE DRIVE

Latigo Shore Drive is one of the first beach areas to be developed
in Malibu, and it rivals Malibu Road for "old time Malibu" status. Rare
turnover among its residents means that neighbors know each other
well. Therefore, it has a quaint, small town feel. It is mostly dry beach
and is known for good surfing as well as its lovely cove, called Latigo
Cove. It is away from PCH and runs along a small road that is not a
through street. There are 35 homes here with one large condominium
complex, which sits above Latigo Shore on Seagull Way. Buying a home
in Latigo is difficult because many of its residents have lived here for
years and are slow to sell.

## 9. MALIBU COVE COLONY

Malibu Cove Colony is the area west of Latigo Shore Drive. Its
main street, Malibu Cove Colony Drive, sits parallel to PCH. A guard
gate protects this neighborhood. Because it has its own street, children
can ride their bikes and play in the neighborhood. In addition, its location away from PCH gives it a cozy, beach community feel. The beach
is partially dry, so during a high tide, there is nowhere to walk along the
shore without getting wet.

## 10. ESCONDIDO BEACH

Escondido Beach is a charming and quaint neighborhood located alongside Malibu Cove Colony. Up the hill from here is Geoffrey's, one of Malibu's best restaurants. Although Escondido Beach and Malibu Cove Colony are located next to each other, they couldn't be more different. The beaches in Escondido Beach are dry. This area is located below PCH and has only single-family homes. Driving and parking here are a challenge because the street is narrow. In Escondido Beach, you'll find mostly full-time residents who have lived here for years. Many of these charming homes are available for summer rentals, but homes are rarely for sale.

## 11. PARADISE COVE

Paradise Cove has some of the most expensive properties in Malibu. This area lies before Pointe Dume. It is set above the beach. Therefore, you must descend stairs or walk down paths to access the ocean. Some properties have small roads that take their residents down to the water.

The homes in Paradise Cove are located on PCH, but they have long driveways that lead away from the busy highway. The lots tend to be larger. In fact, some residents have pools, tennis courts, and horse stables. A few bluff properties have beach cottages in which you can walk down the bluff and relax by the beach. These cottages have been here for years and are located close to the sand.

In addition, Paradise Cove is home to both a pier and a mobile home park. This area's beach is a popular hangout for locals, and it is a tourist attraction as well. The beachfront is dry and expansive; there are miles and miles of private beaches with cliffs and homes above.

## 12. POINTE DUME BLUFFS

Pointe Dume Bluffs dramatically juts into the Pacific. Within this beachfront section there is Pointe Dume and Little Dume. I'll explain the features of both in the paragraphs that follow. Many homes on Pointe Dume Bluffs have direct access to the beach through private or shared entrances. In addition, Cliffside, Grayfox, Zumirez, and Birdview Drives dead end at private gated paths that lead to the beaches below. Birdview is one of the main streets that runs along the bluff. Throughout Pointe Dume, residents treasure their beaches and maintain the beauty of the pathways themselves. Several years ago, along some streets on the Pointe, the beach rights were sold to the State; the beach below is now a public beach and is called Westward Beach. The parcels of land can be an acre or more, and many of the larger homes have pools, tennis courts, and beautiful gardens. Properties here are usually gated. There are no sidewalks, so you'll often see residents taking their dogs for walks along the road, riding horses and bikes, and enjoying magnificent sunsets.

The most striking feature of Big Dume is the whale watching point. The military flattened the top of this hill years ago, and today it's an ideal place to catch views of the California Coast.

Little Dume has many cul-de-sac streets. At the end of the streets are private beaches. Many of the homes were built in the 1960's. Therefore, you may still see ranch-style homes, which were popular to build at the time. Today, some of those homes still exist, but many have been torn down and rebuilt. It is rare to find a vacant parcel of land here, but a few are still available.

## 13. BROAD BEACH

Broad Beach is probably tied with The Colony and Carbon Beach in terms of exclusivity, but it's unlike the other two. This is in large part because of its famous nearby beach. Between Westward Beach and Broad Beach lies Zuma Beach. Zuma is one of the most well-known public beaches in Los Angeles. It has a marvelous, well-maintained shoreline with restrooms and snack shacks. During the week, it's a popular hang-out for nearby Pepperdine University and Malibu High students. Throughout the day, you'll see kids studying on the sand and hanging out with friends.

Zuma Beach's allure has both advantages and disadvantages for nearby residents. On one hand, it is a world-class beach within minutes of their homes. On the other hand, its appeal brings high foot traffic, which can get in the way of its residents' privacy.

Broad Beach has deep sandy knolls and public access entry points. Because of the depth of its lots, homes here can have expansive patios with grassy yards, Jacuzzis, and swimming pools. The properties sit level with the sand. There are small cottages here along with large homes. This area is located on its own road, Broad Beach Road. In addition, there is Sea Level Drive, West Sea Level Drive, La Chusa Point, and newly added Broad Beach Lane.

As you may know, Malibu's beachfront is known for its world-class architecture. On La Chusa Point, you'll find a famous home designed by renowned architect John Lautner. In addition, Sea Level Drive is the beachfront where I sold Hugh and Kimberly Heffner their first beachfront home many years ago.

Throughout Broad Beach, the streets are quiet, and the sand along the coast is superb. This area's residents appreciate that it is located away from PCH, which offers seclusion from the bustling highway. The lots here are deep and wide. Most homes are large, while there are a few smaller beach properties. The beach is mostly dry, and some houses have a small yard along the beachfront. This is the only beach in Malibu that has a combination of ice plants and sand dunes. For this reason, Broad Beach reminds many people of Monterey or Carmel, California.

## 14. EL MATADOR BEACH

Although Pacific Coast Highway is the street address for homes along El Matador Beach, most of the homes here are perched on a bluff above the beach. There are a few properties along the beachfront as well—some that sit on the sand are located along a gated street.

El Matador Beach is open to the public. Therefore, people can walk from the bluff down to the coast. You can reach both El Matador and Broad Beach by walking along the beach from Sea Level Drive. Compared to other areas in Malibu, the beaches are less crowded and are home to beautiful rock formations and caves. In addition to its human residents, whooping cranes call this area home as well.

## 15. ENCINAL BLUFFS

The real estate in Encinal Bluffs is similar to that of Paradise Cove. Therefore, the homes tend to be large and may have an acre or more of land. Some homes are substantial enough to have horse stables. The newer homes, on the other hand, tend to be built on smaller lots.

Encinal Bluffs is above the ocean on the west end of Malibu. Many of its residents live here all year. The homes typically have more property (one or more acres), a PCH address, and stairways that lead down to the beach. Some homes, however, do not have access to the beach below, and permits to build new stairways are not currently available.

## 16. COUNTY LINE

As the name indicates, County Line is on the westernmost part of the city. There are some beachfront homes here as well as two condominium complexes, the Malibu Bay Club, Whaler's Village, and the Leo Carrillo Campground, which is located a bit past the County Line. Although County Line is a charming place to live, 90 percent of beachfront buyers say that it is too far from the Westside of Los Angeles.

## WHERE DO YOU WANT TO LIVE?

With almost 20 communities along Malibu's beachfront, you have many choices to make when buying coastal property. The variation from one area to another, such as the difference between Las Flores and Encinal Bluffs, makes Malibu's beachfront one of the most diverse and interesting places to live in the world.

If you're unfamiliar with Malibu's beachfront, or if you've been a long-time resident and didn't know about the distinct communities along PCH, this chapter has given you an overview of Malibu's coastal property. I suggest you spend a couple of hours on a beautiful Southern California day, drive along PCH, and see if you can identify the different sections along the 27-mile stretch of this city's coast. The more you know about Malibu, the easier you can determine which area will best meet your needs.

# MALIBU'S AGENTS HAVE SEEN IT ALL

As you've read in these pages, the real estate along Malibu's beachfront has qualities that separate it from other areas. From Las Tunas to County Line, each community has features that appeal to its residents for different reasons.

Regardless of whether you're a buyer or seller, your agent must have impeccable rapport skills in order to successfully represent you in your home sale or purchase. In addition, a solid beachfront specialist can potentially make you millions in your real estate investment.

An agent with years of experience will know how to turn difficult situations into ones that work to your advantage. Here's an example a colleague shared with me.

The McGrath's owned a home in exclusive Broad Beach. They had previously lived in the home, but three years prior had relocated to Beverly Hills. Since their move, they had been leasing the home. The real estate market was strong, so they decided to sell their Malibu property. But in the meantime, they continued to lease their home.

Ken was a movie producer in Los Angeles. His primary residence was in the Hollywood Hills. During the summer months of the past three years, he leased homes in Malibu. The previous summer he lived in Broad Beach. As opposed to areas like Carbon Beach and La Costa, he liked how Broad Beach was located away from PCH.

Every evening, he stepped out of his home and walked along the shoreline to watch the sunset at Zuma Beach. Although he enjoyed the Hollywood Hills, after spending a couple of months in Malibu, he realized that he wanted to live by the beach permanently. Unfortunately, home prices were too high for him to buy in Malibu. Nevertheless, he was willing to stretch his finances if he found a home that appealed to him. His agent, Rick, found the McGrath's home and told his client about it.

"Ken, I've found you a home in Broad Beach."

"Tell me about it," Ken said.

"It's a five bedroom 5,000 square foot home. It's on the water and has a swimming pool," he said.

"Is it in good shape?" he said.

"The owners just renovated the house and did a great job. I took a look at it a couple of days ago. Right now they are leasing it for $50,000 per month for the summer, then it will go down to $30,000. But there's another piece of good news about it," he said.

"What?"

"The owners want to sell if they find the right buyer."

"Great. When can we take a look?" he asked

Ken and Rick made an appointment to see the home. After seeing it, Ken knew it was the home he wanted to buy. Unfortunately for him, he still had his home in the Hollywood Hills. He decided to lease the Malibu home for a few months, giving him time to sell his property and decide if he really wanted to extend his finances in order to buy his dream home.

The McGrath's agent, Kelly, met the two and felt confident that Ken would make a good buyer for the home. She consulted with the owners, and they offered to sell it for $7.5 million.

Ken agreed, and the seller drafted a lease agreement that included an option to buy at the end of the year. He moved in the next the month.

As far as his finances were concerned, Ken was a solid candidate to buy the home. Here Kelly made the right choice. Unfortunately, she didn't know what a difficult tenant he would be. From the first week, Ken was as high maintenance as the home's septic system. First, he was not satisfied with the sheets that were left for him. Next, the security system in the home was too difficult to arm and disarm. He also complained that the paint on the exterior was peeling and the water temperature in the shower was not hot enough. Nothing about the home seemed to please him.

The owners were growing tired of having to take care of petty problems, and Kelly was tired of resolving Ken's complaints. In the meantime, since they had signed the one-year lease agreement, property value in Broad Beach had gone up. During Ken's stay, a similar home sold nearby for $9 million as opposed to the $7.5 million the McGrath's agreed to sell the home for. Rick phoned his client to share the good news.

"Ken, I just faxed you something. A home near yours just sold for $9 million," he said.

"Really. What do you think the one I'm in right now is worth?" he asked.

"The house was almost identical in lot size and square footage to yours," he said. "I've been thinking over your lease agreement, and I have an idea. What do you think of buying the home after the lease is up, then flipping it?" he asked.

"You mean that I'll take the McGrath's up on their offer then turn around and sell it for $9 million? Do you really think we can sell it for that much?"

"The market is really hot now. A home almost identical to yours just sold for $9 million. Imagine if you sold the home for the same amount. I think you're in a good position to earn $1.5 million for just leasing a home. How often can a tenant say that he earned that much from renting for a few months?"

"I like your point. What do we do from here?" he asked.

"I'll start looking for buyers," Rick said.

Rick had an extensive list of buyers who were interested in homes along Malibu's beachfront. Word got around that the Broad Beach home would be available for sale at the beginning of the year for $9 million.

The real estate community in Malibu is small, and eventually Kelly, the McGrath's real estate agent, found out that Rick was advertising the Broad Beach home for sale before the lease was even over. This did not please Kelly or her clients.

In addition, the McGrath's did not anticipate that the home would increase in value so much within a matter of months, or they would have certainly agreed to sell the home for more money. But with the lease expiring in a matter of months, and the tenant actively pursuing buyers without even owning the home, what were the owners to do?

Fortunately for the McGrath's, Kelly was a shrewd businessperson. She knew that Rick, Ken's agent, was finding buyers for a home that wasn't even his to sell yet. She consulted with the McGrath's and came up with a plan. It was October, and the lease was due to expire in December. She placed the home on the MLS for $8.5 million. Now, Rick's prospective buyers were seeing the same home for sale for $500,000 less than the price for which he told them they could buy it.

By undercutting his price, Kelly was sending a clear message to Ken: He was going to have a tough time selling the home for $9 million. This made Ken think twice about purchasing the property. Certainly, if he bought the property for $7.5 million and sold it for $8.5 million, he would still make a profit of $1 million. On the other hand, this would be one-third less than his agent's initial sales figure. In addition, with the fluctuating value of property, there was no guarantee that the home would sell for even that much.

Lastly, although Ken definitely made a good living as a movie producer, a $7.5 million home was a significant investment that would leave him with little savings. If he could not sell the home for the price he wanted, he would own a home that he could barely afford.

At the end of the year, Ken's lease was up. Over the last few weeks, the McGrath's were anxious to hear about their tenant's decision. In the end, Kelly's move to list the home on the MLS for $8.5 million gave Ken cold feet. When his lease expired, he moved out of the house and forfeited the option to buy.

Kelly's decision to place the home on the MLS tapped into doubts that Ken had about the Broad Beach home. When she undercut the price that Rick had been advertising, Ken began having second thoughts about his agent's plans.

## LIGHT FIXTURES CAN BREAK $12 MILLION DEALS

The owners of high-end property are typically a very wise group of individuals. Most are shrewd businesspeople and treat people fairly. Once in while, they are shrewd businesspeople who will also try their best to make the transaction as difficult for buyers and their agents as possible.

When you've been in the business for as long as I have, you can tell right away when a client is going to cause trouble. A colleague shares the story of a light fixture that a seller refused to leave in the home.

The $12 million home was on Carbon Beach. The owners had put a tremendous amount of work into the 5,000 square foot residence—it was impeccably maintained and tastefully decorated. The buyers wanted a home that they could move into immediately without having to make any changes. Once they saw the Carbon house, they knew that it was what they wanted.

Upon the close of the sale, the sellers let the buyers know that they were going to take a light fixture with them. The sellers were surprised to hear the news. The fixture was bolted to the ceiling, and its design matched the rest of the bathroom where it was located. The buyers insisted that it was part of the home and that they were entitled to have it once escrow closed.

The sellers maintained that the light fixture was purchased recently. After removing it, they planned to replace it with the original one. If the buyers wanted it, they offered to sell it for $20,000.

The buyer's agent was feeling anxiety over the matter. Both parties were getting upset over a piece of glass, and neither was willing to compromise. Escrow was closing within a week, and the light fixture could have broken the deal. The agent came to the conclusion that when the buyers and sellers of a $12 million dollar home were arguing over a light fixture, the object itself was not really the problem. Furthermore, it was nice, but definitely not worth $20,000 dollars.

After realizing this, the next question the agent asked herself was why the owners would wait until the very end of escrow to announce that they were removing it from the ceiling. The agent came to the conclusion that the owners wanted to get the most out of the deal, and the light fixture was a simple way to do this. Although the amount was a small part of the owners' vast wealth, it was worth $20,000 for them to create a difficult situation for everyone. The agent was in a bind. Her clients refused to pay anything for the light fixture and threatened to walk away from the deal.

In the end, the agent negotiated to pay $10,000 for the fixture herself. The sellers were happy because they earned an extra $10,000 from the $12 million sale. The buyers were pleased because their agent bought the light for them. Finally, the agent was relieved that escrow closed. This was not the first time, nor would it be the last, that she would have to make multi-millionaires happy by buying them such things as $10,000 light fixtures.

Yes, the super-rich can sometimes have egos as expansive as the views from their beachfront homes. Another colleague tells the story of an owner who was dissatisfied with the results of the home inspection.

Tracy, a high-profile film producer from Toronto, made millions from renovating beachfront homes in Malibu. He took great pride in his work and would fly from Canada to oversee the construction of his projects. Often, he would live in the homes as they were being renovated. His current project was a Broad Beach property. Three years prior, he bought it for $3.5 million dollars. The renovation was almost complete, and he was listing the home for $9.5 million.

Brian, a real estate agent, was looking for property for his clients. When he arrived at the Broad Beach home to meet Tracy, a man answered the door. He had the physique of a bodybuilder, and his shoulders seemed to fill the threshold. Brian introduced himself and told him that he was there to meet Tracy. The man led Brian inside. As he was waiting, another man, equally as muscular, walked by. Brian considered himself a healthy man but couldn't help feel somewhat small next to the two super-sized men.

A door from a nearby room opened, and Tracy entered to meet Brian. He too had a gym-chiseled physique, which was obvious since he was wearing only bikini underwear. Brian felt a bit awkward but did his best to hide it. He introduced himself.

"Hello, thank you for allowing me to come over today," he said. He looked around the room, impressed by Tracy's home improvement skill.

"It's a great house isn't it?" Tracy asked.

"It certainly is. You've done a lot of work I can tell," he said.

"Yes, it's definitely been a big project."

Brian was surprised to hear Tracy's voice. By looking at his build, Brian was expecting to hear a booming baritone. Instead, what came out was a squeak that sounded like helium-induced speech.

"Is it ever tough to give up a home that you've put so much work into?" Brian asked.

"Sometimes it is. I take a lot of pride in the work. I have no tolerance for sloppy construction. But I get over it once I make my millions," he said.

Brian walked through the home and was inspired by the high quality of the renovation. For instance, all of the rooms were electronically networked together. Each one had a touch screen remote that controlled the lighting, security, and entertainment systems. By pressing a button on the small remote, the flat panel display in the living room would change from DVD to satellite television to images from the various closed-circuit cameras outside. In addition, the landscaping was impressive, almost as much as the view of the Pacific from the living and master bedrooms.

Brian said good-bye to the movie producer and his entourage of burly men and left the home eager to share his find with his clients. A couple of days later, Brian's clients attended a showing and were immediately convinced that the home was what they wanted. He arranged for the home inspection, certain that Tracy's work would result in a trouble-free report.

The inspection came back to Brian's office. As he imagined, the home was in very good condition. The inspector gave it high marks for its solid construction. The foundation was in good shape and the new septic system worked efficiently. The inspector found only one matter that needed to be addressed. In the upstairs bedroom, the lighting did not respond to the touch screen remote. When Brian showed the inspection to his clients, they requested that Tracy take care of the matter.

Tracy was not happy to hear the news. He insisted that there was no problem with the lighting system. When he tested it, he said that it worked properly. Brian met Tracy again at the home to see for himself. The two walked into the room and Brian reached for the remote. He selected the lighting option on the touch screen, and immediately the room filled with light. But when he attempted it again, the light did not respond to his command. Tracy stood in disbelief. He had no alternative but to find out what was malfunctioning.

The next day, Tracy phoned Brian and told him that the problem was solved. A wire within the bedroom's light fixture needed to be replaced. It was a minor glitch, and he was clearly annoyed that the inspector had pointed it out. Brian arranged for the inspector to visit the house once again to make sure that the light worked.

He and the inspector pulled up to the Broad Beach home. Tracy met them at the door, again, wearing nothing more than a bikini. The three ascended the winding staircase and walked to the bedroom. Tracy pointed out what he did to repair the light.

"It really wasn't a big deal," he said. "Anyone with the slightest ounce of common sense could have fixed this right away."

The inspector took a look and agreed that the light was no longer an issue. On their way out, he handed Tracy his business card.

"Thanks," he said. "I'll be sure to call you if I ever need anything," he smirked at the two, took the card, and used it to pick his teeth.

Once they were fastened in their seatbelts, the inspector told Brian, "I've never met anyone so rude in my life." The two winded their way down PCH. Brian was surprised to hear this, considering that he had enough stories like these to fill a book.

When you buy along Malibu's coast, you are investing in some of the most valuable real estate in the world. After all, with its wide-ranging properties, expansive coastline, and high-profile residents, Malibu's beachfront reputation is well deserved.

As I've shared throughout these pages, it takes a specialized agent to successfully work along Malibu's 27-mile stretch of PCH. The right beachfront agent—one who has exclusive comparables; who has successfully won listings in multiple offer settings; who works honestly and ethically; and who treats others with respect—has the potential to make you millions along Malibu's beachfront. Best wishes to you in fulfilling your dreams to "Buy the Beach."

# ABOUT THE AUTHOR

Katie Bentzen is C.E.O. of Buy the Beach Inc., a real estate company that specializes in Malibu beachfront property. Throughout her 15-year career, Katie has been a top-producing agent in Malibu. Her client list includes Oscar Award winning actors, Lords of England, and ordinary people who love the beach.

## ORDER **BUY** *the* **BEACH** AND
## DISCOVER MORE ABOUT MALIBU

You can purchase *Buy the Beach: How to Make Millions in Malibu Real Estate* online at www.buythebeachinc.com or www.atlasbooks.com/marktplc/01462.htm. To place your order, have your credit card ready.

To find out more about beachfront real estate in Malibu, contact Buy the Beach Inc. online at www.buythebeachinc.com. Once there, you'll see amazing homes, read important real estate information, and learn more about life in The Bu.